PASSIVE INCOME

for Beginners

A Step-by-Step Guide to Building Wealth with Minimal Effort

VINCENZO CORATTI

Copyright © 2024 by VINCENZO CORATTI
All rights reserved.
No part of this book may be reproduced
in any form without the written permission
of the publisher or the author, except as
permitted by USA's copyright law.

Preface

Welcome to "Passive Income for Beginners: A Step-by-Step Guide to Building Wealth with Minimal Effort." Whether you're new to the concept of passive income or looking to expand your existing knowledge, this book is designed to provide you with a comprehensive roadmap to financial independence.

In today's fast-paced world, the pursuit of financial stability and freedom has never been more relevant. Many of us are seeking ways to break free from the traditional 9-to-5 grind, looking for opportunities that allow us to generate income with less direct involvement. This is where passive income comes into play. Passive income streams can provide you with the financial flexibility to pursue your passions, spend more time with loved ones, and enjoy a more balanced and fulfilling life.

This book is divided into ten detailed chapters, each carefully crafted to guide you through different aspects of creating and managing passive income streams. From understanding the basics and setting realistic expectations, to exploring various passive income opportunities such as stock market investments, real estate, affiliate marketing, e-commerce, blogging, online courses, and self-publishing, we cover it all. Each chapter is packed with practical advice, real-life case studies, and actionable steps to help you start building your passive income portfolio today.

One of the core themes you'll find throughout this book is the importance of mindset. Building passive income is not just about finding the right opportunities; it's also about cultivating the right mindset. You'll learn how to develop a growth mindset, stay motivated, and overcome the inevitable setbacks that come with any entrepreneurial endeavor.

In addition to strategies and tips, this book emphasizes the significance of maintaining a balanced life. Achieving financial independence through passive income should enhance your life, not complicate it. You'll discover ways to manage your time effectively, avoid burnout, and enjoy the fruits of your efforts without sacrificing your well-being.

As you embark on this journey, remember that building passive income is a marathon, not a sprint. It requires patience, persistence, and a willingness to continuously learn and adapt. The path may be challenging, but the rewards are well worth the effort. Financial freedom is not just a distant dream; it's a tangible goal that you can achieve with the right knowledge and dedication.

We hope this book serves as a valuable resource and inspiration for you. Our goal is to equip you with the tools and insights needed to create sustainable passive income streams that will pave the way to financial independence and a more fulfilling life.

Thank you for choosing this book as your guide. Now, let's dive in and start building your passive income future!

SUMMARY

Chapter 1: Introduction to Passive Income 8
- 1.1 Definition of Passive Income 8
- 1.2 Why Passive Income Matters 11
- 1.3 Types of Passive Income 15
- 1.4 The Right Mindset for Passive Income 20
- 1.5 Preparing for Success 24

Chapter 2: Stock Market Investments 30
- 2.1 Introduction to Stock Market Investing 30
- 2.2 Passive Investment Strategies 35
- 2.3 Portfolio Diversification 39
- 2.4 Automating Your Investments 44
- 2.5 Monitoring and Adjusting Your Portfolio 49

Chapter 3: Real Estate Investments 56
- 3.1 Introduction to Real Estate Investing 56
- 3.2 Purchasing Property for Passive Income 62
- 3.3 Property Management 67
- 3.4 Investing in REITs (Real Estate Investment Trusts) 72
- 3.5 Real Estate Crowdfunding 77

Chapter 4: Affiliate Marketing 82
- 4.1 Understanding Affiliate Marketing 82
- 4.2 Choosing the Right Affiliate Programs 86
- 4.3 Building an Affiliate Marketing Platform 91
- 4.4 Promoting Affiliate Products 96
- 4.5 Scaling Your Affiliate Marketing Efforts 101

Chapter 5: E-commerce and Dropshipping 107
- 5.1 Introduction to E-commerce 107
- 5.2 Setting Up Your E-commerce Store 111

5.3 Sourcing Products for Dropshipping 116

5.4 Marketing Your E-commerce Store 120

5.5 Automating Your E-commerce Business 125

Chapter 6: Blogging for Passive Income 130

6.1 Starting a Blog 130

6.2 Creating High-Quality Content 135

6.3 Monetizing Your Blog 141

6.4 Building and Engaging Your Audience 146

6.5 Scaling Your Blogging Income 151

Chapter 7: Creating and Selling Online Courses 156

7.1 The Online Course Market 156

7.2 Developing Your Course Content 161

7.3 Choosing the Right Platform 166

7.4 Marketing and Selling Your Course 171

7.5 Scaling Your Online Course Business 176

Chapter 8: Writing and Self-Publishing E-books 183

8.1 Introduction to Self-Publishing 183

8.2 Writing Your E-book 187

8.3 Designing and Formatting Your E-book 192

8.4 Publishing Your E-book 197

8.5 Marketing and Promoting Your E-book 202

Chapter 9: Creating and Monetizing a YouTube Channel 208

9.1 Starting a YouTube Channel 208

9.2 Creating Engaging Video Content 213

9.3 Monetizing Your YouTube Channel 218

9.4 Growing Your YouTube Audience 222

9.5 Diversifying Your YouTube Income 227

Chapter 10: Building a Passive Income Mindset 233

10.1 The Importance of Mindset in Passive Income Success 233

10.2 Setting Realistic Expectations 237

10.3 Staying Motivated and Persistent 241

10.4 Continuous Learning and Adaptation 246

10.5 Creating a Balanced Life 250

Appendix: Summary and Practical Guidelines for Building Passive Income 256

Chapter 1: Introduction to Passive Income

1.1 Definition of Passive Income

Passive income is a term that has gained significant popularity in the financial world. To truly grasp its potential, it is essential to understand what passive income is and how it fundamentally differs from active income. Additionally, recognizing the importance of passive income in achieving financial freedom, along with its advantages and challenges, can provide a clearer perspective on why it is a critical component of a comprehensive financial strategy.

What is Passive Income?

Passive income refers to earnings that require minimal to no effort to maintain once the initial setup is complete. Unlike active income, which is earned through active work or direct involvement (such as salaries, wages, and freelance payments), passive income is generated with little ongoing effort. Examples of passive income include rental income, dividends from stocks, earnings from a blog or YouTube channel, royalties from books or music, and income from online courses.

The primary allure of passive income is the concept of earning money without being actively involved in the daily grind. Once a passive income stream is established, it continues to generate revenue with minimal oversight. This does not mean that passive income requires no effort at all; often, there is significant upfront work involved in setting up these income streams. However, the ongoing maintenance typically demands less time and energy compared to active income sources.

Differences Between Passive and Active Income

The fundamental difference between passive and active income lies in the nature and amount of effort required. Active income is directly tied to the time and effort one puts into their work. For instance, a person working a 9-to-5 job earns a salary that directly corresponds to the hours they work. If they stop working, their income stops as well.

In contrast, passive income is not directly tied to time or active effort. For example, if you own rental properties, the rent collected each month is a form of passive income. Although there might be occasional work involved in maintaining the property or dealing with tenants, it is not a continuous effort that requires your daily attention. Similarly, investments in dividend-yielding stocks generate income through dividends, which are paid out regularly without the need for constant management.

Another significant difference is scalability. Active income is typically limited by the number of hours one can work in a day. Passive income, however, can scale more easily. For instance, once an online course is created, it can be sold to an unlimited number of people without requiring additional work from the creator.

The Importance of Passive Income for Financial Freedom

Financial freedom is often defined as having enough passive income to cover all living expenses, allowing individuals to make decisions based on their interests and passions rather than financial necessity. Passive income plays a crucial role in achieving this state of financial independence.

By building multiple streams of passive income, one can reduce reliance on a single source of active income. This diversification provides a safety net against job loss or other financial setbacks. Moreover, passive income can supplement retirement savings, ensuring a more comfortable and secure future.

Another key benefit of passive income is the potential for time freedom. With active income, individuals are often bound to a schedule or location. Passive income, on the other hand, provides the flexibility to spend time on what truly matters, whether it's pursuing hobbies, traveling, or spending more time with family.

Advantages of Passive Income

1. **Financial Security**: Passive income provides a consistent revenue stream, which can enhance financial stability and reduce stress related to financial uncertainties.

2. **Time Freedom**: With less time required to maintain passive income streams, individuals can allocate their time towards activities they enjoy or furthering other financial ventures.

3. **Scalability**: Passive income has the potential to grow exponentially. Once established, many passive income sources can be scaled up without a proportional increase in effort.

4. **Diversification**: Having multiple streams of passive income can protect against market volatility and economic downturns. This diversification reduces risk and increases overall financial resilience.

5. **Legacy Building**: Many forms of passive income, such as real estate or intellectual property, can be passed down to future generations, providing long-term benefits for your family.

Challenges of Passive Income

1. **Initial Effort and Investment**: Setting up passive income streams often requires significant time, effort, and financial investment upfront. This can be a barrier for many people.

2. **Maintenance and Management**: While passive income requires less ongoing effort than active income, it is not entirely hands-off. Regular maintenance and occasional troubleshooting are often necessary.

3. **Risk and Uncertainty**: All investments come with risks. Market fluctuations, property values, and other economic factors can affect the stability and amount of passive income.

4. **Learning Curve**: Successfully generating passive income requires knowledge and skills in various areas, such as investing, real estate, or online business. This learning curve can be steep and time-consuming.
5. **Patience and Perseverance**: Building substantial passive income streams takes time. It requires patience and a long-term perspective, as significant returns are often not immediate.

Understanding the nuances of passive income, its importance in achieving financial freedom, and the associated advantages and challenges provides a solid foundation for anyone looking to enhance their financial strategy.

1.2 Why Passive Income Matters

Understanding the significance of passive income is crucial for anyone looking to achieve long-term financial stability and independence. Passive income can play a pivotal role in your financial planning by providing continuous cash flow, reducing reliance on active income sources, and offering the freedom to pursue your passions without the constraints of traditional employment.

The Significance of Passive Income in Long-Term Financial Planning

Passive income is a cornerstone of robust financial planning because it diversifies income sources and builds financial resilience. Unlike active income, which ceases when you stop working, passive income continues to flow even if you are not actively involved. This ongoing revenue stream is vital for several reasons:

1. **Risk Mitigation**: Diversifying your income streams reduces the risk associated with relying solely on one source of income. In the event of a job loss or economic

downturn, having multiple streams of passive income can provide a financial cushion.

2. **Wealth Accumulation**: Passive income allows for the accumulation of wealth over time. When reinvested, these earnings can compound, leading to exponential growth in your net worth.

3. **Financial Independence**: The ultimate goal for many is to achieve financial independence—having enough income to cover living expenses without needing to work actively. Passive income is instrumental in reaching this goal, as it generates revenue with minimal ongoing effort.

To illustrate, consider the following chart that demonstrates the growth potential of passive income compared to active income over time. The chart assumes a starting point where both active and passive incomes are equal, but the passive income is reinvested.

How Passive Income Can Free Up Your Time

One of the most appealing aspects of passive income is the freedom it offers. Time is a finite resource, and passive income allows you to leverage your time more effectively. Here are several ways passive income can liberate your schedule:

1. **Reduced Work Hours**: With a steady stream of passive income, you may not need to work as many hours in a traditional job. This reduction can free up time for personal interests, hobbies, or family.

2. **Flexible Lifestyle**: Passive income can provide the flexibility to live life on your own terms. Whether it's traveling the world, pursuing a passion project, or simply enjoying more leisure time, passive income can make it possible.

3. **Less Stress**: Financial stress is a significant burden for many people. Knowing that you have a stable source of income independent of your job can alleviate this stress, leading to a better quality of life.

To provide a clearer picture, let's look at a case study of a successful passive income earner.

Case Studies of Successful Passive Income Earners

Case Study 1: Sarah's Real Estate Empire

Sarah, a 45-year-old marketing executive, began investing in real estate in her early 30s. She started with a small rental property, which she purchased using savings and a mortgage. Over the years, she reinvested the rental income to acquire more properties. Today, Sarah owns ten rental properties, generating enough passive income to cover all her living expenses. Her journey highlights several key points:

- **Initial Investment**: Sarah's initial investment in her first property required significant savings and a willingness to take on debt.
- **Reinvestment Strategy**: By reinvesting her rental income, Sarah was able to expand her property portfolio without needing additional outside capital.
- **Financial Freedom**: Sarah's passive income from her properties now allows her to pursue other interests, such as travel and philanthropy, without worrying about her financial stability.

Case Study 2: John's Digital Products

John, a software engineer, created a series of online courses and eBooks on programming and web development. He launched his first course on a popular e-learning platform and, over time, added more content. Today, John earns a substantial passive income from course sales and royalties. Key takeaways from John's experience include:

- **Leveraging Expertise**: John utilized his professional skills to create valuable content that others are willing to pay for.

- **Scalability**: Digital products have a high scalability factor, allowing John to reach a global audience with minimal additional effort.

- **Ongoing Revenue**: Once the courses were created, they continued to generate income with little need for continuous updates, providing John with a reliable revenue stream.

Case Study 3: Emily's Dividend Investing

Emily, a financial analyst, focused on building a portfolio of dividend-paying stocks. She carefully selected companies with a history of consistent dividend payouts and reinvested those dividends to buy more shares. Over a decade, Emily's portfolio grew substantially, and the dividend income now provides her with a significant portion of her annual earnings. Highlights from Emily's strategy include:

- **Long-Term Focus**: Emily's approach required patience and a long-term perspective, as the benefits of dividend investing compound over time.

- **Reinvestment**: By reinvesting dividends, Emily was able to accelerate the growth of her investment portfolio.

- **Stability**: Dividend-paying stocks tend to be from established, stable companies, providing Emily with a reliable income stream.

These case studies illustrate the diverse paths one can take to achieve financial freedom through passive income. Whether through real estate, digital products, or dividend investing, the common thread is the strategic planning and dedication required to establish and grow passive income streams. By understanding and leveraging the power of passive income, you can create a more secure and flexible financial future.

1.3 Types of Passive Income

Exploring the different types of passive income is essential for understanding how to diversify and optimize your earnings. Each type of passive income has its unique characteristics, benefits, and challenges, making some more suitable for certain individuals than others. Here, we delve into various passive income streams, examining their pros and cons and identifying who might benefit most from each type.

Overview of Different Types of Passive Income

Investments

Investments in the stock market, bonds, and other financial instruments are classic forms of passive income. These can include dividends from stocks, interest from bonds, and returns from mutual funds or ETFs.

- **Dividends from Stocks**: Companies distribute a portion of their profits to shareholders in the form of dividends.
- **Interest from Bonds**: Bonds pay interest at regular intervals, providing a steady income stream.
- **Mutual Funds and ETFs**: These investment vehicles pool money from many investors to purchase a diversified portfolio of stocks, bonds, or other securities.

Real Estate

Real estate is another popular source of passive income. This can include rental properties, real estate investment trusts (REITs), and crowdfunding platforms that pool investments for property purchases.

- **Rental Properties**: Owning residential or commercial properties and renting them out to tenants.
- **REITs**: Publicly traded companies that own, operate, or finance income-producing real estate.

- **Crowdfunding**: Platforms that allow investors to pool their money to fund real estate projects.

Online Ventures

The digital age has opened numerous opportunities for passive income through online ventures. These include blogging, affiliate marketing, creating digital products, and YouTube channels.

- **Blogging**: Earning money through ads, sponsored posts, and affiliate marketing.
- **Affiliate Marketing**: Promoting products or services and earning a commission on sales made through your referral links.
- **Digital Products**: Selling eBooks, online courses, and software.
- **YouTube**: Generating revenue through ad views, sponsorships, and merchandise sales.

Pros and Cons of Each Type

Investments

Pros:

- **Scalability**: Investments can grow significantly over time with compounding returns.
- **Liquidity**: Stocks and bonds can be sold relatively quickly if needed.
- **Diversification**: Broad range of options to spread risk.

Cons:

- **Market Risk**: Subject to market fluctuations and economic downturns.
- **Knowledge Requirement**: Requires understanding of financial markets and investment strategies.
- **Initial Capital**: Significant capital might be required to generate meaningful income.

Real Estate

Pros:

- **Stable Income**: Rental properties provide consistent monthly income.
- **Appreciation**: Property values can increase over time, adding to wealth.
- **Tax Benefits**: Various tax deductions available for property owners.

Cons:

- **Management Effort**: Requires time and effort to manage properties or deal with property managers.
- **Liquidity**: Real estate is not as easily liquidated as stocks or bonds.
- **Market Risk**: Property values can decline due to market conditions.

Online Ventures

Pros:

- **Low Startup Cost**: Many online ventures require minimal initial investment.
- **Scalability**: Potential to reach a global audience with digital products and content.
- **Flexibility**: Can be managed from anywhere with an internet connection.

Cons:

- **Time-Intensive Setup**: Building an online presence and generating traffic can take significant time and effort.
- **Unpredictable Income**: Earnings can fluctuate based on market trends and audience engagement.

- **Constant Updates**: Digital content and strategies need regular updating to remain relevant.

Which Types Might Be Best Suited for Different People

Choosing the right type of passive income depends on various factors, including individual skills, available capital, risk tolerance, and time commitment.

For Risk-Averse Individuals

- **Bonds and Dividend Stocks**: These provide more predictable returns and lower risk compared to other investments.
- **REITs**: Offer real estate exposure with less management effort and risk.

For Those with Time and Technical Skills

- **Online Ventures**: Blogging, affiliate marketing, and creating digital products can be ideal for tech-savvy individuals with time to invest upfront.

For Those with Significant Capital

- **Real Estate**: Buying rental properties or investing in real estate crowdfunding requires substantial initial investment but can yield consistent returns.
- **High-Value Stocks and Mutual Funds**: Investing in a diversified portfolio can provide steady growth and income.

For Busy Professionals

- **Robo-Advisors and ETFs**: Automated investment services that manage portfolios with minimal effort required.
- **REITs and Crowdfunding Platforms**: Provide real estate exposure without the need to manage properties directly.

Example Table of Passive Income Types

Passive Income Type	Pros	Cons	Best For
Dividends from Stocks	Scalable, Liquid, Diversified	Market Risk, Knowledge Requirement	Risk-Averse, Capital Ready
Rental Properties	Stable Income, Appreciation, Tax Benefits	Management Effort, Liquidity, Market Risk	Capital Ready, Risk Tolerant
Blogging	Low Startup Cost, Scalable, Flexible	Time-Intensive Setup, Unpredictable Income	Tech-Savvy, Time Available
REITs	Less Management, Diversified, Stable	Market Risk, Lower Control	Risk-Averse, Busy Professionals
Digital Products	Low Startup Cost, Scalable, Flexible	Time-Intensive Setup, Constant Updates	Tech-Savvy, Creative

Understanding the different types of passive income, their advantages, and challenges, as well as aligning them with your personal situation, is crucial for making informed decisions. This approach ensures that you build a diversified and resilient portfolio of passive income streams tailored to your financial goals and lifestyle preferences.

1.4 The Right Mindset for Passive Income

To successfully generate passive income, having the right mindset is as crucial as having the right strategy. Developing an entrepreneurial mindset, overcoming the fear of risk and uncertainty, and understanding the importance of patience and perseverance are key components in this journey. These mental shifts can empower you to navigate the challenges and seize the opportunities that passive income presents.

Developing an Entrepreneurial Mindset

An entrepreneurial mindset is characterized by innovation, creativity, and a willingness to take calculated risks. It involves seeing opportunities where others see obstacles and being proactive in creating value. Here are some ways to cultivate this mindset:

1. **Embrace Learning and Growth**:
   - Continuous learning is fundamental. Entrepreneurs thrive on acquiring new knowledge and skills. Engage in reading, take online courses, and attend workshops related to your areas of interest in passive income.
   - Stay updated on market trends and technological advancements that can impact your income streams.

2. **Be Solution-Oriented**:
   - Focus on solving problems and meeting needs. Whether it's through creating a product, providing a service, or investing wisely, your aim should be to add value.
   - Innovative thinking often leads to new and lucrative passive income opportunities.

3. **Adaptability and Flexibility**:
   - The ability to adapt to changing circumstances is essential. The economic environment, market trends, and personal

circumstances can shift, and an entrepreneurial mindset helps you pivot and adjust your strategies accordingly.

- Being flexible allows you to explore new ventures and adjust existing ones to maximize returns.

4. **Goal Setting and Planning**:

- Clear, actionable goals give direction to your efforts. Set short-term and long-term objectives and create a roadmap to achieve them.

- Break down your goals into manageable tasks and regularly review and adjust your plans to stay on track.

Overcoming Fear of Risk and Uncertainty

Risk and uncertainty are inherent in any entrepreneurial endeavor, and passive income ventures are no exception. However, overcoming this fear is crucial for success. Here are strategies to manage and mitigate risk:

1. **Education and Research**:

- The more you know, the less you fear. Educate yourself thoroughly about the passive income streams you are interested in. Understanding the risks involved and how to mitigate them reduces fear and builds confidence.

- Conduct comprehensive research before making any investments or starting a new venture.

2. **Risk Management Strategies**:

- Diversification is a key risk management tool. Spread your investments across different assets to minimize the impact of any single investment's poor performance.

- Use financial tools such as insurance and hedging to protect against significant losses.

3. **Start Small and Scale Gradually**:

- Begin with small investments or projects to build experience and confidence. As you gain more knowledge and see positive results, you can gradually increase your investment.

- This approach helps in learning from mistakes without suffering significant financial setbacks.

4. **Seek Mentorship and Advice**:

- Connect with mentors and peers who have experience in generating passive income. Their insights and advice can help you navigate uncertainties and avoid common pitfalls.

- Join forums, networks, and communities where you can share experiences and learn from others.

The Importance of Patience and Perseverance

Building substantial passive income streams takes time. Patience and perseverance are essential virtues in this process. Here's why they matter:

1. **Long-Term Perspective**:

- Passive income ventures, especially those involving investments or real estate, often require a long-term perspective. Immediate returns are rare; the benefits accrue over time.

- Having a long-term vision helps in staying committed and focused despite short-term challenges and fluctuations.

2. **Consistency and Persistence**:

- Regular, consistent efforts are more effective than sporadic bursts of activity. Whether it's contributing to an investment fund, updating a blog, or managing rental properties, consistent effort is key to building and maintaining income streams.

- Perseverance in the face of setbacks ensures that temporary failures do not derail your overall goals.

3. **Managing Expectations**:

- Understand that building passive income is not a get-rich-quick scheme. Unrealistic expectations can lead to frustration and abandonment of efforts. Set realistic milestones and celebrate incremental successes.
- Patience allows you to ride out the inevitable ups and downs and stay the course toward long-term success.

4. **Learning from Failures**:

- Failure is often part of the journey. Each setback provides valuable lessons that can inform and improve your future efforts.
- View failures as learning opportunities rather than final outcomes. This mindset fosters resilience and continuous improvement.

Example Table: Entrepreneurial Mindset vs. Traditional Employee Mindset

Aspect	Entrepreneurial Mindset	Traditional Employee Mindset
Learning	Continuous, self-driven	Limited to job requirements
Risk Tolerance	Embraces calculated risks	Avoids risks, prefers stability
Goal Setting	Sets ambitious, flexible goals	Focuses on short-term, fixed goals

Aspect	Entrepreneurial Mindset	Traditional Employee Mindset
Adaptability	Highly adaptable to change	Resistant to change, prefers routine
Problem Solving	Seeks innovative solutions	Follows established procedures

Developing the right mindset for passive income involves embracing an entrepreneurial spirit, managing risks intelligently, and exercising patience and perseverance. These mental attributes are as vital as financial strategies in creating sustainable and scalable passive income streams. By cultivating these traits, you can navigate the complexities of passive income generation and move closer to achieving financial independence and freedom.

1.5 Preparing for Success

Achieving success in generating passive income requires meticulous preparation, including setting clear financial goals, creating a detailed action plan, and continuously monitoring progress while adapting strategies as needed. These steps are critical to ensuring that your passive income ventures are effective and sustainable.

Setting Clear and Realistic Financial Goals

The foundation of any successful passive income strategy begins with setting clear, realistic financial goals. These goals should be specific, measurable, achievable, relevant, and time-bound (SMART).

1. **Specific**:
   - Define what you want to achieve in precise terms. Instead of a vague goal like "make more money," specify "generate $1,000 per month in passive income within two years."
   - Detail the sources of this income, such as "through rental properties and dividend stocks."

2. **Measurable**:
   - Ensure that your goals can be quantified. This allows you to track progress and determine when you have achieved them.
   - Use metrics like monthly income, percentage returns, or number of income streams.

3. **Achievable**:
   - Set goals that are challenging yet attainable based on your current financial situation, knowledge, and resources.
   - Consider your starting point and incremental steps needed to reach your goals.

4. **Relevant**:
   - Your goals should align with your broader financial aspirations and personal values. For example, if financial independence is your ultimate aim, your passive income goals should contribute directly to this objective.
   - Ensure that each goal supports your overall strategy and long-term vision.

5. **Time-Bound**:
   - Assign a timeline to your goals to create a sense of urgency and a framework for tracking progress.
   - Set short-term milestones (e.g., six months, one year) and long-term targets (e.g., five years).

Creating a Detailed Action Plan

Once you have established your goals, the next step is to create a detailed action plan. This plan should outline the specific steps you need to take to achieve your goals, including the resources required and timelines for completion.

1. **Identify Resources and Skills Needed**:

- Determine what resources (financial, educational, time) and skills you need to achieve your goals.
- This might include savings for initial investments, knowledge in real estate or stock markets, and time for research and management.

2. **Develop Step-by-Step Actions**:

- Break down your goals into smaller, manageable tasks. For example, if your goal is to invest in rental properties, your action plan might include:

3. Researching profitable real estate markets.
4. Securing financing or saving for a down payment.
5. Identifying and purchasing a property.
6. Finding tenants and managing the property.

7. **Set Timelines for Each Task**:

- Assign deadlines to each task to ensure steady progress and keep yourself accountable.
- Use tools like Gantt charts or project management software to visualize timelines and dependencies.

8. **Allocate Resources Wisely**:

- Budget your finances and time effectively to ensure you can complete each task without overextending yourself.

- Consider hiring experts or using professional services for complex tasks such as legal advice or property management.

9. **Anticipate Challenges and Plan Contingencies**:

- Identify potential obstacles and develop contingency plans. For instance, what will you do if a property purchase falls through or if the market fluctuates?
- Being prepared for setbacks ensures that you can quickly adapt and continue moving forward.

Monitoring Progress and Adapting Strategies

Ongoing monitoring and flexibility in adapting your strategies are crucial components of a successful passive income plan. This ensures that you remain on track and can respond to changes in the market or personal circumstances.

1. **Regularly Review Progress**:

- Schedule regular reviews of your progress towards your goals. Monthly or quarterly reviews can help you stay on track.
- Use financial statements, income reports, and other metrics to assess your progress.

2. **Track Key Performance Indicators (KPIs)**:

- Identify and track KPIs relevant to your passive income streams, such as rental yield, dividend yield, or website traffic.
- Comparing these KPIs against your goals can highlight areas where you are excelling or falling short.

3. **Adjust Strategies Based on Performance**:

- If you are not meeting your goals, analyze why and adjust your strategies accordingly. For example, if rental income is lower than expected, you might need to revise your tenant screening process or consider property upgrades.

- Be open to pivoting to new opportunities if your current strategies are not yielding desired results.

4. **Stay Informed and Educated**:

- Keep up with market trends, economic news, and new opportunities in the passive income space.

- Continuous learning ensures that you can adapt your strategies to changing conditions and take advantage of new passive income opportunities.

5. **Celebrate Milestones and Reassess Goals**:

- Recognize and celebrate when you achieve milestones. This can provide motivation and reinforce your commitment to your passive income journey.

- Periodically reassess your goals to ensure they remain relevant and adjust them as your financial situation and aspirations evolve.

Example Action Plan Table

Goal	Task	Deadline	Resources Needed	Potential Challenges
Generate $1,000/month from rentals	Research markets	3 months	Time, real estate courses	Finding reliable data
	Secure financing	6 months	Savings, mortgage approval	Loan approval process

Goal	Task	Deadline	Resources Needed	Potential Challenges
	Purchase property	9 months	Down payment	Competitive market conditions
	Find tenants	12 months	Time, advertising budget	High vacancy rates
	Manage property	Ongoing	Property manager	Maintenance issues

Preparing for success in passive income generation requires clear goal setting, meticulous planning, and diligent monitoring. By following these steps, you can create a structured pathway to financial independence and ensure your efforts are both effective and sustainable.

Chapter 2: Stock Market Investments

2.1 Introduction to Stock Market Investing

Investing in the stock market is a powerful tool for generating passive income and building long-term wealth. To effectively leverage this tool, it is essential to understand what the stock market is, how it functions, the benefits it offers, and the risks involved.

What is the Stock Market and How Does It Work?

The stock market is a collection of markets and exchanges where the buying, selling, and issuance of shares of publicly held companies occur. It serves as a platform where investors can trade equity securities, such as stocks, bonds, and derivatives. The most well-known stock exchanges in the United States are the New York Stock Exchange (NYSE) and the NASDAQ.

Functioning of the Stock Market

1. **Stock Issuance**:

   - Companies issue stocks to raise capital. This process is known as an Initial Public Offering (IPO). Through an IPO, a company sells shares to the public for the first time.

   - Investors who buy these shares become partial owners of the company and are entitled to a portion of its profits, usually paid as dividends.

2. **Trading of Stocks**:

   - Once a company's shares are listed on an exchange, they can be bought and sold by investors. The stock market operates on a continuous auction basis, where buyers and sellers place orders to buy or sell stocks.

- The price of a stock is determined by supply and demand. If more people want to buy a stock than sell it, the price goes up, and vice versa.

3. **Market Participants**:

- **Individual Investors**: Private individuals who buy and sell stocks.
- **Institutional Investors**: Organizations such as mutual funds, pension funds, and insurance companies that invest large sums of money in the stock market.
- **Market Makers**: Firms that provide liquidity by buying and selling stocks at publicly quoted prices.

4. **Stock Indices**:

- Indices like the S&P 500, Dow Jones Industrial Average, and NASDAQ Composite track the performance of a group of stocks, providing a benchmark for the market's overall performance.

Benefits of Investing in the Stock Market

Investing in the stock market offers several significant advantages that can enhance your financial portfolio and provide a reliable source of passive income.

1. **Potential for High Returns**:

- Historically, the stock market has provided higher returns compared to other investment vehicles such as bonds or savings accounts. Over the long term, stocks have outperformed most other assets.
- Compounded returns on reinvested dividends and capital gains can significantly increase wealth over time.

2. **Dividend Income**:

- Many companies pay dividends to their shareholders, providing a steady stream of income. Dividend-paying stocks can be an excellent source of passive income.

- Dividends can be reinvested to purchase more shares, leading to exponential growth through the power of compounding.

3. **Liquidity**:

- Stocks are relatively liquid investments. This means they can be easily bought and sold with minimal transaction costs, providing flexibility to investors.

- This liquidity allows investors to quickly convert their holdings into cash if needed.

4. **Diversification**:

- The stock market offers a wide range of investment opportunities across various industries and sectors. This diversity allows investors to spread their risk and reduce the impact of poor performance in any single investment.

- Diversified portfolios tend to be more stable and can weather market volatility better.

5. **Ownership and Voting Rights**:

- Stock ownership grants shareholders a stake in the company, including voting rights on important corporate matters. This can be particularly beneficial if you invest in companies you believe in or are passionate about.

Risks Associated with Stock Investments

While the stock market can provide substantial benefits, it also comes with risks that investors must understand and manage.

1. **Market Volatility**:
   - Stock prices can be highly volatile, with prices fluctuating significantly in response to economic data, corporate performance, geopolitical events, and market sentiment.
   - Short-term volatility can lead to significant losses if stocks are sold at a low point.

2. **Economic Factors**:
   - The stock market is influenced by broader economic conditions, such as inflation rates, interest rates, and economic growth. Adverse economic conditions can negatively impact stock prices.
   - Global events, such as trade wars or pandemics, can also affect market stability and investor confidence.

3. **Company-Specific Risks**:
   - Individual stocks carry the risk of poor company performance due to management decisions, competitive pressures, or industry downturns.
   - Negative news, such as accounting scandals or product recalls, can lead to sharp declines in stock prices.

4. **Market Timing**:
   - Successfully timing the market—buying low and selling high—is notoriously difficult. Many investors fall victim to emotional decision-making, buying during market peaks and selling during downturns.
   - Long-term investment strategies typically yield better results than attempting to time the market.

5. **Liquidity Risk**:
   - While stocks are generally liquid, some stocks, especially those of smaller companies, may have lower trading

volumes, making them harder to sell quickly without affecting the price.

Example Table: Pros and Cons of Stock Market Investing

Aspect	Pros	Cons
Potential Returns	High long-term returns	High short-term volatility
Dividend Income	Steady income stream	Dividends are not guaranteed
Liquidity	Easy to buy and sell	Can lead to impulsive trading
Diversification	Spread risk across sectors	Requires research and monitoring
Ownership Rights	Voting rights and a stake in the company	Exposure to company-specific risks
Economic Sensitivity	Growth linked to economic expansion	Vulnerable to economic downturns
Market Timing	Long-term strategies can compound returns	Difficult to time the market accurately

Understanding the dynamics of the stock market, recognizing its benefits, and being aware of its risks are fundamental to making informed investment decisions. By doing so, you can harness the power of stock market investing to build a robust portfolio that supports your passive income goals.

2.2 Passive Investment Strategies

Passive investment strategies are designed to maximize returns over the long term with minimal active management and effort. By understanding the principles of long-term investing versus active trading, leveraging index funds and ETFs, and selecting the right funds for your portfolio, you can effectively build and sustain passive income streams.

Long-term Investing vs. Active Trading

Investors can choose between long-term investing and active trading, each with distinct approaches, benefits, and risks.

Long-term Investing

Long-term investing involves buying and holding assets for an extended period, typically years or decades, to benefit from compound growth and market appreciation.

1. **Compound Growth**:

- Over time, the value of investments can grow exponentially due to compounding returns. Reinvesting dividends and capital gains leads to a snowball effect, significantly increasing wealth.

- The chart below illustrates the potential growth of a $10,000 investment over 20 years with a 7% annual return:

2. **Reduced Stress and Effort**:

- Long-term investors avoid the stress of daily market fluctuations and the need for constant monitoring and trading. This approach aligns well with a passive income strategy, focusing on steady, sustained growth.

3. **Lower Costs**:

- By minimizing the frequency of transactions, long-term investing reduces trading fees and capital gains taxes, enhancing overall returns.

4. **Historical Performance**:
   - Historically, long-term investments in diversified portfolios have consistently outperformed short-term trading strategies, particularly when factoring in transaction costs and taxes.

Active Trading

Active trading involves frequently buying and selling securities to capitalize on short-term market movements. This approach requires significant time, expertise, and resources.

1. **Higher Potential Returns**:
   - Active traders aim to outperform the market by taking advantage of short-term price fluctuations. Successful traders can achieve higher returns than the market average.

2. **Increased Risk and Stress**:
   - Active trading is highly demanding and stressful, requiring constant market monitoring and rapid decision-making. It also carries higher risks due to market volatility and the potential for significant losses.

3. **Higher Costs**:
   - Frequent trading incurs substantial transaction fees and higher tax liabilities, which can erode profits.

Index Funds and ETFs as Passive Investment Tools

Index funds and exchange-traded funds (ETFs) are popular passive investment vehicles that offer broad market exposure, diversification, and cost-efficiency.

Index Funds

Index funds are mutual funds designed to replicate the performance of a specific market index, such as the S&P 500. They provide broad exposure to the market, enabling investors to benefit from overall market growth.

1. **Diversification**:
   - Index funds invest in a wide range of securities within the index, reducing the impact of poor performance by individual stocks.

2. **Low Costs**:
   - Index funds typically have lower expense ratios compared to actively managed funds because they simply track an index without frequent trading.

3. **Consistent Performance**:
   - By mirroring the performance of a benchmark index, index funds provide reliable returns that match overall market trends.

ETFs

ETFs are similar to index funds but trade on stock exchanges like individual stocks. They offer flexibility, liquidity, and low costs, making them ideal for passive investors.

1. **Liquidity**:
   - ETFs can be bought and sold throughout the trading day at market prices, providing greater flexibility compared to mutual funds, which are priced once daily.

2. **Tax Efficiency**:
   - ETFs are generally more tax-efficient than mutual funds due to their unique structure, which minimizes capital gains distributions.

3. **Variety**:
   - ETFs cover a wide range of asset classes, sectors, and geographies, allowing investors to tailor their portfolios to specific investment goals and risk tolerances.

How to Choose the Right Funds for Your Portfolio

Selecting the right index funds or ETFs for your portfolio involves evaluating several factors to ensure they align with your investment objectives and risk tolerance.

1. **Investment Goals**:

- Define your investment goals, such as capital appreciation, income generation, or risk diversification. Choose funds that align with these objectives.

2. **Expense Ratios**:

- Compare the expense ratios of different funds. Lower expense ratios mean lower costs and higher net returns over time.

3. **Performance History**:

- Review the historical performance of the fund relative to its benchmark index. Consistent performance in line with the index indicates a well-managed fund.

4. **Asset Allocation**:

- Ensure the fund's asset allocation aligns with your risk tolerance and investment strategy. For example, a portfolio focused on growth might favor equity funds, while a conservative portfolio might include more bond funds.

5. **Fund Size and Liquidity**:

- Larger funds tend to be more stable and liquid, making them easier to buy and sell without affecting the market price.

6. **Tracking Error**:

- Assess the tracking error, which measures how closely the fund's performance matches its benchmark index. Lower tracking errors indicate better alignment with the index.

Example Table: Comparison of Index Funds and ETFs

Feature	Index Funds	ETFs
Trading	Priced once daily	Trades throughout the day
Liquidity	Less liquid	Highly liquid
Expense Ratios	Generally low	Very low
Tax Efficiency	Less efficient	More efficient
Investment Minimums	Often has minimum investment amounts	Typically no minimum investment

By adopting passive investment strategies such as long-term investing and leveraging tools like index funds and ETFs, you can build a diversified and cost-effective portfolio that supports sustainable passive income. Careful selection of the right funds tailored to your financial goals and risk tolerance is crucial to maximizing returns and achieving financial independence.

2.3 Portfolio Diversification

Diversification is a fundamental principle of investing, essential for managing risk and ensuring the stability of your investment portfolio. By spreading investments across different asset classes, sectors, and geographical regions, you can mitigate the impact of poor performance in any single area. This section will explore the importance of diversification, strategies to diversify your portfolio, and the tools and resources available to monitor and balance your investments effectively.

The Importance of Diversification for Risk Management

Diversification involves spreading your investments across various assets to reduce exposure to any single asset or risk. This strategy helps to:

1. **Minimize Risk**:

- Diversification reduces the impact of a decline in any one investment. If one asset class underperforms, gains in another can offset losses, smoothing overall portfolio performance.

2. **Enhance Returns**:

- While diversification primarily aims to manage risk, it can also enhance returns by including a mix of assets that perform well under different economic conditions.

3. **Reduce Volatility**:

- A diversified portfolio typically experiences less volatility compared to a concentrated one. This stability can provide peace of mind and make it easier to stay invested during market fluctuations.

4. **Protect Against Uncertainty**:

- Financial markets are inherently unpredictable. Diversification provides a buffer against unexpected events that could negatively impact specific sectors or regions.

Strategies to Diversify Your Investment Portfolio

Effective diversification requires a strategic approach to selecting and balancing investments. Here are some key strategies:

1. **Asset Class Diversification**:

- Spread investments across different asset classes such as stocks, bonds, real estate, and commodities. Each asset class responds differently to economic conditions, providing a balanced risk-return profile.

Asset Class	Typical Characteristics
Stocks	High growth potential, higher volatility
Bonds	Lower risk, steady income
Real Estate	Potential for income and appreciation, illiquid
Commodities	Hedge against inflation, highly volatile

2. **Sector Diversification**:

- Within each asset class, diversify across various sectors. For example, in a stock portfolio, include companies from technology, healthcare, consumer goods, finance, and energy sectors. Different sectors perform differently based on economic cycles and specific events.

3. **Geographical Diversification**:

- Invest in a mix of domestic and international markets. This helps protect against country-specific risks and allows you to benefit from growth in different regions.

4. **Investment Styles**:

- Combine growth and value investments. Growth investments focus on companies expected to grow at an above-average rate, while value investments focus on companies undervalued by the market. This balance can enhance returns and reduce risk.

5. **Time Diversification**:

- Use dollar-cost averaging to invest regularly over time, reducing the risk of investing a large amount in a single market peak. This strategy involves buying a fixed dollar amount of an investment at regular intervals, regardless of the share price.

Tools and Resources to Monitor and Balance Your Portfolio

Maintaining a diversified portfolio requires regular monitoring and rebalancing to ensure it remains aligned with your investment goals. Here are some tools and resources to help:

1. **Portfolio Tracking Software**:

   - Use online tools and apps to track your investments' performance, analyze asset allocation, and monitor diversification. Popular options include Personal Capital, Morningstar, and Mint.

2. **Robo-Advisors**:

   - Robo-advisors like Betterment, Wealthfront, and Vanguard Digital Advisor offer automated portfolio management services. They use algorithms to create and maintain a diversified portfolio based on your risk tolerance and goals.

3. **Financial Advisors**:

   - Consulting with a financial advisor can provide personalized advice and help you navigate complex investment decisions. Advisors can offer insights into optimal diversification strategies and assist with portfolio rebalancing.

4. **Investment Platforms**:

   - Many investment platforms offer tools for diversification analysis and portfolio rebalancing. Look for features like asset allocation models, performance reports, and automatic rebalancing.

5. **Regular Reviews**:

   - Schedule periodic reviews of your portfolio to assess performance and make necessary adjustments. Consider rebalancing if your asset allocation drifts significantly from your target due to market movements.

Example Table: Diversification Strategies

Strategy	Description	Benefits
Asset Class Diversification	Investing in a mix of stocks, bonds, real estate, and commodities	Reduces exposure to risk in any single asset class
Sector Diversification	Spreading investments across different sectors	Mitigates sector-specific risks
Geographical Diversification	Investing in domestic and international markets	Protects against country-specific economic downturns
Investment Styles	Combining growth and value investments	Balances potential for high returns with stability
Time Diversification	Investing regularly over time (dollar-cost averaging)	Reduces risk of investing at a market peak

Monitoring and Balancing Example

Consider a portfolio initially balanced with 60% stocks, 30% bonds, and 10% real estate. Over time, due to the stock market's strong performance, the allocation shifts to 70% stocks, 20% bonds, and 10% real estate. This drift increases the portfolio's risk profile beyond the investor's comfort level.

Rebalancing Steps:

1. **Assess Current Allocation**:
   - Use portfolio tracking software to determine the current asset allocation.

2. **Set Rebalancing Thresholds**:
   - Establish thresholds for rebalancing (e.g., if any asset class deviates by more than 5% from the target allocation).

3. **Rebalance Portfolio**:
   - Sell a portion of the overperforming asset (stocks) and reinvest in underperforming assets (bonds) to restore the target allocation.

4. **Regular Monitoring**:
   - Schedule quarterly or annual reviews to ensure the portfolio remains aligned with investment goals and risk tolerance.

By implementing these diversification strategies and using appropriate tools to monitor and balance your portfolio, you can effectively manage risk and enhance the potential for long-term returns. Diversification is a dynamic process that requires regular attention, but the benefits in terms of risk management and financial stability are well worth the effort.

2.4 Automating Your Investments

Automating your investments can be a game-changer for those looking to generate passive income with minimal effort. By leveraging robo-advisor platforms, you can streamline the investment process, reduce costs, and maintain a diversified portfolio without the need for constant oversight. This section will explore how to use robo-advisor platforms, the benefits of automating your investments, and provide examples of popular platforms and how they work.

How to Use Robo-Advisor Platforms

Robo-advisors are automated platforms that provide financial planning services with minimal human intervention. They use algorithms and data analysis to create and manage investment portfolios based on individual goals and risk tolerance. Here's a step-by-step guide on how to use these platforms:

1. **Sign Up and Set Up Your Account**:

- Choose a robo-advisor platform and sign up for an account. You'll need to provide personal information and financial details.

- Complete a questionnaire that assesses your financial goals, investment horizon, and risk tolerance. This information helps the robo-advisor design a tailored investment strategy.

2. **Deposit Funds**:

- Link your bank account to the robo-advisor platform and transfer funds. Some platforms have a minimum investment requirement, so ensure you meet the initial deposit criteria.

3. **Portfolio Creation**:

- Based on your responses to the questionnaire, the robo-advisor will suggest an investment portfolio. This typically includes a mix of asset classes such as stocks, bonds, and sometimes alternative investments like real estate or commodities.

4. **Automated Investing**:

- Once your portfolio is created and funded, the robo-advisor will automatically invest your money according to the selected asset allocation. The platform continuously monitors and rebalances your portfolio to maintain the desired risk level.

5. **Ongoing Management**:

- The robo-advisor provides continuous oversight, adjusting the portfolio as needed based on market conditions and your financial goals. This includes rebalancing the portfolio and reinvesting dividends.

Benefits of Automating Your Investments

Automating your investments through a robo-advisor offers several advantages:

1. **Convenience and Time-Saving**:

- Automation reduces the need for constant monitoring and decision-making, saving you time and effort. The platform handles all aspects of portfolio management, from asset allocation to rebalancing.

2. **Consistency and Discipline**:

- Automated investing ensures consistent contributions and adherence to your investment strategy. It eliminates emotional decision-making and market timing errors, which can negatively impact returns.

3. **Cost-Effectiveness**:

- Robo-advisors typically charge lower fees than traditional financial advisors. These platforms use technology to reduce overhead costs, passing the savings on to investors.

4. **Diversification and Risk Management**:

- Robo-advisors create diversified portfolios tailored to your risk tolerance. They automatically rebalance the portfolio to maintain the desired asset allocation, managing risk effectively.

5. **Accessibility**:

- Many robo-advisors have low minimum investment requirements, making them accessible to a wide range of investors. This democratizes access to professional portfolio management.

Examples of Popular Platforms and How They Work

Several robo-advisor platforms have gained popularity for their ease of use, cost-effectiveness, and reliable performance. Here are some well-known examples:

1. **Betterment**:

   - **How It Works**: Betterment offers goal-based investing, allowing users to set specific financial goals such as retirement, buying a home, or saving for education. The platform creates a personalized portfolio based on these goals and automatically adjusts the asset allocation over time.

   - **Features**: Tax-efficient investing, automatic rebalancing, retirement planning tools, and socially responsible investing options.

   - **Fees**: Betterment charges a management fee of 0.25% per year for its Digital plan and 0.40% per year for its Premium plan, which includes access to human advisors.

2. **Wealthfront**:

   - **How It Works**: Wealthfront uses Modern Portfolio Theory to design diversified portfolios based on users' risk tolerance and financial goals. It offers a range of investment options, including stocks, bonds, real estate, and commodities.

   - **Features**: Tax-loss harvesting, direct indexing, financial planning tools, and a high-interest cash account.

   - **Fees**: Wealthfront charges a management fee of 0.25% per year.

3. **Vanguard Personal Advisor Services**:

   - **How It Works**: Vanguard combines automated portfolio management with access to human financial advisors. This hybrid approach provides personalized advice and ongoing management tailored to individual needs.

- **Features**: Comprehensive financial planning, goal-based investing, and low-cost index funds.

- **Fees**: Vanguard charges a management fee of 0.30% per year for assets under management.

4. **Acorns**:

- **How It Works**: Acorns focuses on micro-investing by rounding up users' everyday purchases to the nearest dollar and investing the spare change. It's designed for beginner investors looking to build wealth gradually.

- **Features**: Round-ups, recurring investments, retirement accounts, and a cash-back program with partner companies.

- **Fees**: Acorns charges a monthly fee ranging from $1 to $5, depending on the plan.

Example Table: Comparison of Robo-Advisors

Feature	Betterment	Wealthfront	Vanguard Personal Advisor Services	Acorns
Management Fee	0.25% - 0.40%	0.25%	0.30%	$1 - $5 per month
Minimum Investment	None	$500	$50,000	None
Tax-Loss Harvesting	Yes	Yes	No	No

Feature	Betterment	Wealthfront	Vanguard Personal Advisor Services	Acorns
Human Advisor Access	Premium Plan Only	No	Yes	No
Special Features	Goal-based investing	Direct indexing	Comprehensive financial planning	Micro-investing

Automating your investments through robo-advisors offers a streamlined, efficient, and cost-effective way to build and manage your investment portfolio. These platforms democratize access to professional investment management, allowing you to achieve your financial goals with minimal effort and lower costs. By understanding how to use these tools, you can take full advantage of their benefits and set yourself on the path to financial independence.

2.5 Monitoring and Adjusting Your Portfolio

Regularly monitoring and adjusting your portfolio is a critical aspect of successful investing. By keeping a close eye on your investments and making necessary adjustments based on market conditions and personal goals, you can ensure that your portfolio remains aligned with your financial objectives. This section explores the importance of portfolio monitoring, tools and techniques for tracking investment performance, and guidelines for making adjustments.

The Importance of Regularly Monitoring Your Portfolio

1. **Ensuring Alignment with Financial Goals**:

- Regular monitoring helps ensure that your portfolio remains aligned with your short-term and long-term financial goals. Changes in personal circumstances or market conditions might necessitate adjustments to maintain alignment.

- Monitoring allows you to track progress towards specific financial milestones, such as retirement, buying a home, or funding education.

2. **Managing Risk**:

- The risk profile of your investments can change over time due to market fluctuations and changes in asset values. Regular reviews help you maintain an appropriate level of risk that matches your risk tolerance.

- By monitoring your portfolio, you can identify and mitigate potential risks before they become significant problems.

3. **Identifying Underperformance**:

- Regular performance reviews help identify underperforming assets. This can prompt timely decisions to rebalance or replace these investments with better-performing alternatives.

- Continuous assessment ensures that your portfolio is optimized for maximum returns.

4. **Rebalancing**:

- Over time, the allocation of assets in your portfolio can drift from your target allocation due to differential growth rates. Regular monitoring helps you rebalance your portfolio to maintain the desired asset mix.

- Rebalancing ensures that your portfolio remains diversified and aligned with your investment strategy.

Tools and Techniques for Tracking Investment Performance

Several tools and techniques can help you effectively monitor your portfolio and track investment performance:

1. **Portfolio Tracking Software**:

- Use portfolio tracking software to get a comprehensive view of your investments. Tools like Personal Capital, Morningstar, and Mint offer features such as performance analysis, asset allocation breakdowns, and tracking against benchmarks.
- These platforms provide real-time updates and alerts, helping you stay informed about market movements and portfolio changes.

2. **Robo-Advisors**:

- Many robo-advisors offer built-in tracking and reporting features. They automatically monitor your portfolio and provide detailed performance reports, making it easier to manage your investments.
- Robo-advisors like Betterment and Wealthfront offer dashboards that show performance metrics, risk assessments, and portfolio health checks.

3. **Brokerage Accounts**:

- Most online brokerage platforms provide tools to track and analyze your portfolio. They offer performance reports, charts, and graphs to help visualize your investments' progress.
- Features like trade history, dividend tracking, and tax reporting are also available to assist in comprehensive portfolio management.

4. **Financial News and Analysis**:

- Stay updated with financial news and market analysis through resources like Bloomberg, CNBC, and The Wall Street Journal. These sources provide insights into market trends, economic indicators, and investment strategies.

- Regularly reading financial news helps you understand the broader market context affecting your investments.

5. **Spreadsheet Tracking**:

- For those who prefer a hands-on approach, maintaining a spreadsheet can be an effective way to track your portfolio. Customize the spreadsheet to include columns for asset type, purchase price, current value, dividends, and overall performance.

- Spreadsheets offer flexibility in how you track and analyze your data, allowing you to tailor it to your specific needs.

When and How to Adjust Your Portfolio Based on Market Conditions

1. **Rebalancing Your Portfolio**:

- **When to Rebalance**: Consider rebalancing your portfolio at regular intervals, such as quarterly or annually. Additionally, rebalance if any asset class deviates significantly from your target allocation (e.g., by more than 5%).

- **How to Rebalance**: To rebalance, sell overperforming assets and buy underperforming ones to restore the desired allocation. Alternatively, adjust your contributions to direct new investments into underweighted asset classes.

2. **Responding to Economic Changes**:

- **Market Conditions**: Pay attention to macroeconomic indicators such as interest rates, inflation, and GDP growth. These factors can affect the performance of different asset classes.

- **Adjustments**: If economic conditions suggest a prolonged downturn, consider shifting to more defensive investments like bonds or utilities. Conversely, in a booming economy, you might increase exposure to growth stocks.

3. **Adapting to Personal Circumstances**:

- **Life Events**: Major life events such as marriage, having children, or nearing retirement can impact your financial goals and risk tolerance. Adjust your portfolio to reflect these changes.

- **Risk Tolerance**: As you age or your financial situation evolves, your risk tolerance may change. Shift your asset allocation to match your current risk appetite, typically moving towards more conservative investments as you approach retirement.

4. **Performance Review**:

- **Underperformance**: If certain investments consistently underperform compared to their benchmarks or peers, consider replacing them with better-performing alternatives.

- **New Opportunities**: Stay open to new investment opportunities that align with your goals and risk tolerance. Emerging sectors or asset classes can offer attractive returns.

Example Table: Portfolio Monitoring Tools Comparison

Tool/Platform	Features	Pros	Cons
Personal Capital	Performance tracking, asset allocation, retirement planning	Comprehensive analysis, user-friendly interface	Higher fees for advisory services
Morningstar	Investment research, portfolio analysis, benchmarks	Detailed insights, extensive research tools	Subscription required for premium features
Mint	Budgeting, spending tracking, investment tracking	Free, integrates with multiple accounts	Limited investment analysis
Betterment	Automated investing, performance reports, tax-loss harvesting	Easy to use, low fees, tax-efficient	Limited human advisor access
Spreadsheet Tracking	Customizable, flexible analysis	Fully tailored to user needs	Time-consuming, requires manual updates

Regularly monitoring and adjusting your portfolio is essential for maintaining alignment with your financial goals, managing risk, and optimizing returns. By using the right tools and techniques, you can stay informed about your investments and make timely adjustments based on market conditions and personal circumstances. This proactive approach ensures that your portfolio remains robust, resilient, and on track to achieve your long-term financial objectives.

Chapter 3: Real Estate Investments

3.1 Introduction to Real Estate Investing

Investing in real estate is a proven method for generating passive income and building long-term wealth. Understanding the fundamentals of real estate investing, including the different types of investments, the associated risks and benefits, and the strategies for adjusting your portfolio based on market conditions, is crucial for success.

Why Invest in Real Estate?

1. **Stable Income**:
- Real estate investments, particularly rental properties, provide a steady and predictable income stream. Monthly rent payments can offer a reliable cash flow, which can be particularly attractive for those seeking financial stability.

2. **Appreciation**:
- Over time, real estate properties tend to increase in value. This appreciation can significantly enhance the return on investment, especially in desirable locations with growing demand.

3. **Tax Benefits**:
- Real estate investors can take advantage of various tax deductions, including mortgage interest, property taxes, and depreciation. These deductions can offset income and reduce overall tax liability.

4. **Inflation Hedge**:
- Real estate is often considered a good hedge against inflation. As inflation rises, so do property values and rental income, helping to preserve the purchasing power of your investment.

5. **Leverage**:
   - Real estate allows investors to use leverage, meaning you can purchase properties with a combination of your own money and borrowed funds. This can amplify returns, though it also increases risk.

Types of Real Estate Investments

1. **Residential Properties**:
   - **Single-Family Homes**: Investing in single-family homes involves purchasing properties to rent to individuals or families. These properties are typically easier to manage and finance.
   - **Multi-Family Homes**: These include duplexes, triplexes, and apartment buildings. Multi-family properties can generate higher rental income and offer economies of scale in management and maintenance.

2. **Commercial Properties**:
   - **Office Buildings**: Investing in office spaces can provide long-term leases with businesses, offering stable income. However, they can be sensitive to economic cycles.
   - **Retail Properties**: Shopping centers and retail stores can yield high returns, especially in prime locations. However, the rise of e-commerce has added some uncertainty to this sector.
   - **Industrial Properties**: Warehouses and distribution centers are in high demand, particularly with the growth of online shopping and logistics. These properties typically have long-term leases and lower maintenance costs.

3. **Real Estate Investment Trusts (REITs)**:
   - **Equity REITs**: These REITs invest in and own properties, generating income from rent and property sales. They offer high liquidity as they are traded on major stock exchanges.

- **Mortgage REITs**: These REITs invest in mortgages and mortgage-backed securities, earning income from the interest on these loans.
- **Hybrid REITs**: These combine both equity and mortgage investments, providing a diversified income stream.

Risks and Benefits of Real Estate Investments

Benefits:

1. **Income Generation**:
   - Rental income provides a steady cash flow, which can be particularly beneficial during retirement or periods of low economic activity.

2. **Diversification**:
   - Real estate can diversify your investment portfolio, reducing overall risk by spreading investments across different asset classes.

3. **Appreciation Potential**:
   - Properties often increase in value over time, providing capital gains when sold.

4. **Tax Advantages**:
   - Various tax benefits, including depreciation and interest deductions, can significantly enhance the net returns from real estate investments.

Risks:

1. **Market Volatility**:
   - Real estate markets can be volatile and subject to economic cycles, affecting property values and rental income.

2. **Liquidity Risk**:
   - Real estate is not as liquid as stocks or bonds. Selling a property can take time and may incur significant transaction costs.

3. **Management Challenges**:
   - Managing rental properties can be time-consuming and requires dealing with tenant issues, maintenance, and vacancies. Hiring a property manager can mitigate this but adds to the cost.

4. **Leverage Risk**:
   - While leverage can amplify returns, it also increases the risk. If property values decline or rental income decreases, meeting mortgage payments can become challenging.

When and How to Adjust Your Portfolio Based on Market Conditions

1. **Market Analysis**:
   - Regularly assess market conditions to determine the optimal times for buying or selling properties. Key indicators include local economic conditions, employment rates, and housing supply and demand.

2. **Diversification**:
   - Diversify your real estate investments across different property types and locations to mitigate risk. This approach helps protect against downturns in specific markets or sectors.

3. **Rebalancing**:
   - Periodically review and rebalance your portfolio to maintain the desired asset allocation. If certain investments outperform, they may constitute a larger proportion of your portfolio, increasing risk.

4. **Economic Indicators**:

- Monitor economic indicators such as interest rates, inflation, and GDP growth. Rising interest rates, for instance, can increase borrowing costs, affecting the profitability of leveraged investments.

5. **Exit Strategies**:

- Develop and implement exit strategies to sell underperforming properties or those in declining markets. Consider the tax implications and potential reinvestment opportunities when selling assets.

Example Table: Types of Real Estate Investments

Investment Type	Characteristics	Benefits	Risks
Single-Family Homes	Owned and rented to individual families	Easier to finance/manage, stable income	High vacancy risk, lower rental income
Multi-Family Homes	Includes duplexes, triplexes, apartment buildings	Higher income, economies of scale	More complex management, higher upfront cost
Office Buildings	Leased to businesses	Long-term leases, stable income	Economic cycle sensitivity, high vacancy rates

Investment Type	Characteristics	Benefits	Risks
Retail Properties	Includes shopping centers, stores	High returns, prime locations	E-commerce impact, consumer behavior changes
Industrial Properties	Includes warehouses, distribution centers	Long leases, low maintenance	Location dependency, economic shifts
Equity REITs	Owns and operates income-generating properties	High liquidity, diversified income	Market volatility, management fees
Mortgage REITs	Invests in mortgages, mortgage-backed securities	Interest income, diversification	Interest rate risk, credit risk

Investing in real estate offers numerous benefits, from steady income to tax advantages and potential for appreciation. However, it also comes with risks that must be carefully managed through diversification, regular market analysis, and strategic portfolio adjustments. By understanding the different types of real estate investments and their unique characteristics, you can make informed decisions that align with your financial goals and risk tolerance.

3.2 Purchasing Property for Passive Income

Investing in property for passive income can be a highly effective strategy for building wealth and achieving financial stability. This section explores the critical steps in purchasing property for passive income, including how to find and evaluate properties, financing real estate purchases, calculating the return on investment (ROI), and adjusting your portfolio based on market conditions.

How to Find and Evaluate Properties

Finding the right property is the first and most crucial step in real estate investing. Here are some strategies to locate and assess potential properties:

1. **Research the Market**:

- Start by researching different markets to understand local economic conditions, population growth, and real estate trends. Websites like Zillow, Realtor.com, and local real estate listings provide valuable market data.

- Look for areas with strong job growth, good schools, low crime rates, and a high demand for rentals.

2. **Use a Real Estate Agent**:

- Engage a local real estate agent who has in-depth knowledge of the market and can help identify promising properties.

- Agents can provide insights into neighborhoods, property values, and potential rental income.

3. **Evaluate the Property**:

- **Location**: Consider the property's proximity to amenities such as schools, shopping centers, public transport, and employment hubs. A desirable location can attract tenants and ensure low vacancy rates.

- **Condition**: Inspect the property thoroughly or hire a professional inspector to identify any structural issues or necessary repairs. A well-maintained property reduces the risk of unexpected expenses.

- **Potential for Appreciation**: Assess the potential for property value appreciation based on market trends and planned infrastructure developments.

4. **Analyze Comparable Sales (Comps)**:

- Compare the property with similar properties that have recently sold in the same area. This helps determine a fair market value and ensures you don't overpay.

Financing Real Estate Purchases

Securing financing is a critical step in real estate investing. Here are common financing options and considerations:

1. **Conventional Mortgages**:

- These are standard home loans offered by banks and mortgage lenders. They typically require a down payment of 20% of the property's value and have fixed or adjustable interest rates.

2. **FHA Loans**:

- Backed by the Federal Housing Administration, these loans require lower down payments (as low as 3.5%) and are easier to qualify for, especially for first-time investors.

3. **Portfolio Loans**:

- These are offered by local banks and credit unions and are kept in the lender's portfolio instead of being sold on the secondary market. They can be more flexible in terms of qualification and terms.

4. **Hard Money Loans**:
   - Provided by private investors or companies, these loans are based on the property's value rather than the borrower's creditworthiness. They have higher interest rates and shorter terms, making them suitable for quick purchases and renovations.

5. **Cash Purchases**:
   - If you have sufficient funds, purchasing property outright can avoid interest payments and speed up the buying process. However, it ties up significant capital that could be used for other investments.

Calculating the Return on Investment (ROI)

Understanding the potential ROI is essential for evaluating the profitability of a real estate investment. Here's how to calculate it:

1. **Gross Rental Income**:
   - Calculate the total annual rental income expected from the property. For example, if the monthly rent is $1,500, the annual rental income is $1,500 x 12 = $18,000.

2. **Operating Expenses**:
   - Deduct all operating expenses, including property management fees, maintenance, property taxes, insurance, and utilities. For example, if these expenses total $6,000 annually, the net rental income is $18,000 - $6,000 = $12,000.

3. **Net Operating Income (NOI)**:
   - NOI = Gross Rental Income - Operating Expenses. In this example, the NOI is $12,000.

4. **Capitalization Rate (Cap Rate)**:

- Cap Rate = (NOI / Property Purchase Price) x 100. If the property was purchased for $200,000, the cap rate is ($12,000 / $200,000) x 100 = 6%.

5. **Cash on Cash Return**:

- This measures the annual return on the actual cash invested. If you invested $40,000 (down payment and closing costs), Cash on Cash Return = (Annual Cash Flow / Total Cash Invested) x 100. Assuming an annual cash flow of $12,000, the return is ($12,000 / $40,000) x 100 = 30%.

When and How to Adjust Your Portfolio Based on Market Conditions

Market conditions can change, affecting the performance of your real estate investments. Here are strategies for adjusting your portfolio:

1. **Regular Market Analysis**:

- Continuously monitor local and national real estate trends, interest rates, and economic indicators. Websites like Realtor.com, Zillow, and industry reports provide valuable insights.
- Adjust your investment strategy based on this analysis, such as shifting focus from residential to commercial properties if the market favors commercial real estate.

2. **Rebalancing**:

- Periodically review your portfolio to ensure it aligns with your investment goals and risk tolerance. Rebalance by selling underperforming properties and reinvesting in higher-potential assets.
- Consider diversifying across different property types and geographical locations to spread risk.

3. **Exit Strategies**:
   - Develop exit strategies for each investment. This might include selling properties in declining markets or those that have reached peak value.
   - Be prepared to reinvest proceeds into new opportunities that align better with current market conditions.

4. **Leveraging Equity**:
   - If property values increase, consider leveraging the equity by refinancing or taking out a home equity loan to invest in additional properties.
   - Ensure that the additional investments align with your overall strategy and risk tolerance.

Example Table: ROI Calculation

Description	Amount ($)
Annual Rental Income	$18,000
Operating Expenses	$6,000
Net Operating Income	$12,000
Property Purchase Price	$200,000
Cap Rate	6%
Total Cash Invested	$40,000
Annual Cash Flow	$12,000
Cash on Cash Return	30%

Purchasing property for passive income involves thorough research, careful evaluation, strategic financing, and ongoing portfolio management. By following these steps, you can build a robust real estate portfolio that provides steady income and long-term growth, adapting to market changes and maximizing your investment returns.

3.3 Property Management

Effective property management is crucial for maximizing income from real estate investments. This involves employing strategies for property management, ensuring proper maintenance and cost management, utilizing property management services, and knowing when and how to adjust your portfolio based on market conditions.

Strategies for Managing Properties to Maximize Income

1. **Screen Tenants Carefully**:

- Thorough tenant screening can significantly reduce the risk of non-payment and property damage. Check credit scores, verify employment and income, and review rental history.

- Use comprehensive tenant applications and conduct in-person interviews to ensure you select reliable tenants.

2. **Set Competitive Rental Rates**:

- Research local rental markets to set competitive rates. Pricing too high can lead to vacancies, while pricing too low can reduce potential income.

- Adjust rental rates periodically based on market conditions, inflation, and property improvements.

3. **Implement Efficient Rent Collection Processes**:

   - Use automated systems for rent collection to ensure timely payments. Platforms like Rentec Direct, Cozy, and Buildium offer online payment solutions.
   - Enforce late fees consistently to encourage on-time payments.

4. **Regularly Review and Renew Leases**:

   - Conduct lease reviews to ensure terms are up-to-date and aligned with current market conditions. Consider adding clauses that protect against inflation and allow for periodic rent increases.
   - Renew leases with reliable tenants to maintain stable occupancy rates.

5. **Maintain High Occupancy Rates**:

   - Minimize vacancies by offering incentives for lease renewals, such as minor upgrades or rent discounts.
   - Market your property effectively through online listings, social media, and real estate agents to attract potential tenants quickly.

The Importance of Maintenance and Cost Management

1. **Preventative Maintenance**:

   - Regular maintenance prevents small issues from becoming major problems. Create a maintenance schedule for HVAC systems, plumbing, roofing, and other critical areas.
   - Conduct routine inspections to identify and address issues promptly.

2. **Cost Management**:

   - Control expenses by obtaining multiple quotes for repairs and maintenance work. Negotiate contracts with service providers to secure the best rates.

   - Keep detailed records of all expenses to track spending and identify areas for cost-saving measures.

3. **Property Improvements**:

   - Invest in property improvements that increase value and rental appeal. Upgrades such as modern appliances, energy-efficient windows, and updated flooring can attract higher-paying tenants.

   - Balance the cost of improvements with the potential increase in rental income to ensure a positive ROI.

4. **Energy Efficiency**:

   - Implement energy-efficient solutions to reduce utility costs. This can include installing LED lighting, energy-efficient appliances, and proper insulation.

   - Consider offering green initiatives, such as recycling programs or solar panels, which can attract environmentally conscious tenants.

Using Property Management Services

1. **Benefits of Professional Management**:

   - Property management companies handle day-to-day operations, including tenant screening, rent collection, maintenance, and lease management. This reduces the workload for property owners.

   - Professional managers have expertise in local markets and can optimize rental income and occupancy rates.

2. **Selecting a Property Management Company**:

   - Research and compare property management companies to find one that suits your needs. Consider factors such as experience, fees, services offered, and reputation.

   - Interview multiple companies and request references to ensure they have a track record of effective property management.

3. **Cost of Property Management Services**:

   - Property management fees typically range from 8% to 12% of the monthly rental income. Additional fees may apply for leasing, maintenance, and other services.

   - Evaluate the cost-benefit ratio to determine if professional management will enhance overall returns.

4. **Communication and Reporting**:

   - Establish clear communication channels with your property manager. Regular updates and detailed reports on property performance, finances, and maintenance issues are essential.

   - Ensure the management company provides transparent accounting practices and easy access to financial statements.

When and How to Adjust Your Portfolio Based on Market Conditions

1. **Market Analysis**:

   - Continuously monitor real estate market trends, including vacancy rates, rental prices, and economic indicators. This helps identify opportunities and risks.

   - Use tools like Zillow, Realtor.com, and local market reports for up-to-date information.

2. **Rebalancing Your Portfolio**:

- Periodically review your property portfolio to ensure it aligns with your investment goals and risk tolerance. Rebalance by selling underperforming properties and reinvesting in high-potential markets.

- Diversify your holdings across different property types and locations to mitigate risk.

3. **Exit Strategies**:

- Develop clear exit strategies for each investment. Consider selling properties in declining markets or those that have appreciated significantly to reinvest in more promising opportunities.

- Evaluate tax implications and potential reinvestment opportunities before selling assets.

4. **Leveraging Market Conditions**:

- Take advantage of favorable market conditions, such as low-interest rates, to refinance properties or acquire new investments.

- During economic downturns, focus on retaining high-quality tenants and maintaining stable occupancy rates.

Example Table: Property Management Strategies

Strategy	Benefits	Implementation Tips
Tenant Screening	Reduces risk of non-payment and damage	Use comprehensive applications, conduct interviews
Competitive Rental Rates	Ensures high occupancy rates	Research market rates, adjust regularly

Strategy	Benefits	Implementation Tips
Efficient Rent Collection	Timely payments, reduces late payments	Use automated systems, enforce late fees
Regular Lease Reviews	Keeps terms current, allows rent increases	Periodic reviews, add inflation clauses
Preventative Maintenance	Prevents major repairs, extends property life	Schedule regular inspections, address issues promptly
Energy Efficiency	Reduces utility costs, attracts tenants	Install efficient appliances, offer green initiatives

Effective property management is essential for maximizing rental income and ensuring the long-term success of your real estate investments. By implementing strategic management practices, maintaining properties proactively, leveraging professional management services, and adjusting your portfolio based on market conditions, you can enhance your investment returns and build a robust real estate portfolio.

3.4 Investing in REITs (Real Estate Investment Trusts)

Real Estate Investment Trusts (REITs) provide an accessible and diversified way to invest in real estate without the need to own or manage physical properties. This section will explore what REITs are and how they work, the benefits of investing in REITs, and how to choose the right REITs for your portfolio.

What is a REIT and How Does It Work?

1. **Definition of a REIT**:
   - A REIT is a company that owns, operates, or finances income-producing real estate across various property sectors. REITs allow individual investors to buy shares in commercial real estate portfolios, which receive income from a variety of properties.

2. **Types of REITs**:
   - **Equity REITs**: These REITs own and operate income-producing real estate. They generate revenue primarily through leasing space and collecting rents on the properties they own.
   - **Mortgage REITs (mREITs)**: These REITs provide financing for income-producing real estate by purchasing or originating mortgages and mortgage-backed securities. They earn income from the interest on these financial assets.
   - **Hybrid REITs**: These REITs combine the investment strategies of both equity REITs and mortgage REITs, holding both properties and mortgages.

3. **How REITs Work**:
   - REITs pool capital from multiple investors to purchase and manage a portfolio of real estate assets. This structure allows individual investors to earn a share of the income produced without having to buy, manage, or finance any properties themselves.
   - REITs are required to pay out at least 90% of their taxable income to shareholders in the form of dividends, which provides a steady income stream.

Benefits of Investing in REITs

1. **Diversification**:
   - REITs offer a way to diversify an investment portfolio by adding real estate exposure. This diversification helps spread risk, as real estate markets often do not move in tandem with stock or bond markets.

2. **Liquidity**:
   - Unlike direct real estate investments, REITs are traded on major stock exchanges, making them highly liquid. Investors can buy and sell shares easily, just like stocks.

3. **Income Generation**:
   - REITs typically offer attractive dividend yields, as they are required to distribute the majority of their income to shareholders. This makes them a good option for income-focused investors.

4. **Professional Management**:
   - REITs are managed by experienced real estate professionals who handle the acquisition, management, and disposal of properties. This professional management can lead to better investment outcomes compared to individual property ownership.

5. **Accessibility**:
   - Investing in REITs requires significantly less capital than direct real estate investments. This accessibility allows a broader range of investors to gain exposure to real estate markets.

How to Choose the Right REITs for Your Portfolio

1. **Evaluate the REIT's Property Portfolio**:
   - Examine the types of properties the REIT invests in and their locations. Look for REITs with properties in high-

demand areas and sectors that are likely to experience growth (e.g., industrial properties, data centers).
- Assess the diversity of the portfolio. A well-diversified REIT will have properties across different sectors and geographical regions, which can mitigate risk.

2. **Assess Financial Performance**:
- Review the REIT's historical financial performance, focusing on metrics such as Funds From Operations (FFO), net operating income (NOI), and dividend yield. FFO is a key measure of a REIT's operating performance and its ability to generate income.
- Look at the REIT's payout ratio to ensure it is sustainable. A very high payout ratio might indicate potential cash flow issues, while a lower ratio might suggest room for dividend growth.

3. **Management Quality**:
- Investigate the experience and track record of the REIT's management team. Effective management is crucial for making strategic property acquisitions, maintaining high occupancy rates, and managing costs.
- Consider the governance structure and whether management's interests are aligned with those of shareholders. Look for REITs where management holds a significant equity stake.

4. **Market and Sector Trends**:
- Analyze the trends and outlook for the specific sectors in which the REIT operates. For example, consider how e-commerce growth impacts retail REITs versus industrial REITs.
- Stay informed about broader economic factors that affect real estate markets, such as interest rates, economic growth, and demographic trends.

5. **Risk Factors**:

- Assess the risks associated with the REIT, including market risk, interest rate risk, and the potential for tenant default. Diversification within the REIT's portfolio can mitigate some of these risks.

- Review the REIT's debt levels. High leverage can increase risk, especially in an environment of rising interest rates.

Example Table: Comparing Different Types of REITs

Type of REIT	Income Source	Benefits	Risks
Equity REITs	Rent from properties	Steady income, potential for property appreciation	Market risk, property-specific risks, economic downturns
Mortgage REITs	Interest on mortgage loans	High dividend yields, diversification from property ownership	Interest rate risk, credit risk, prepayment risk
Hybrid REITs	Combination of rent and interest	Diversified income sources	Combined risks of equity and mortgage REITs

Investing in REITs can be a strategic addition to your investment portfolio, offering exposure to real estate markets with the benefits of liquidity, professional management, and regular income. By carefully evaluating REITs based on their property portfolio, financial performance, management quality, market trends, and risk factors, you can make informed decisions that align with your investment goals and risk tolerance. This approach ensures that your REIT investments contribute effectively to your overall strategy for building sustainable passive income.

3.5 Real Estate Crowdfunding

Real estate crowdfunding has emerged as a popular investment strategy, allowing individual investors to pool their money to fund real estate projects and share in the profits. This section will introduce real estate crowdfunding platforms, discuss the advantages and disadvantages of crowdfunding, and provide guidance on how to get started.

Introduction to Real Estate Crowdfunding Platforms

Real estate crowdfunding platforms connect investors with real estate developers seeking capital for their projects. These platforms offer a variety of investment opportunities, including residential, commercial, and mixed-use properties. Here's how they work:

1. **Platform Mechanics**:

- **Fundraising Campaigns**: Real estate developers list their projects on crowdfunding platforms, detailing the investment requirements, projected returns, and timeframes.

- **Investor Participation**: Investors browse available projects, select those that align with their investment goals, and contribute funds.

- **Pooling Resources**: Funds from multiple investors are pooled to meet the capital requirements of the listed projects.

- **Returns Distribution**: Investors receive returns based on their share of the investment, typically through rental income, interest payments, or profit from property sales.

2. **Types of Crowdfunding Investments**:
   - **Equity Investments**: Investors purchase shares in a property or development project, earning a return from rental income and property appreciation.
   - **Debt Investments**: Investors lend money to real estate developers, earning fixed interest payments over the loan term. These are often less risky but offer lower returns compared to equity investments.
3. **Popular Crowdfunding Platforms**:
   - **Fundrise**: Offers a range of investment options, including eREITs and individual properties, with low minimum investment requirements.
   - **RealtyMogul**: Provides both equity and debt investment opportunities, including commercial and residential properties.
   - **CrowdStreet**: Focuses on commercial real estate projects, offering institutional-grade investments to accredited investors.

Advantages and Disadvantages of Crowdfunding

Advantages:

1. **Accessibility**:
   - Crowdfunding platforms lower the barriers to real estate investment, allowing individuals to invest with relatively small amounts of capital. This democratizes access to real estate markets.
2. **Diversification**:
   - Investors can diversify their portfolios by investing in a variety of properties across different geographical locations and property types, thereby spreading risk.

3. **Passive Income**:
   - Real estate crowdfunding provides a source of passive income through regular rental payments or interest income from debt investments. Investors do not need to manage properties directly.

4. **Professional Management**:
   - Projects listed on crowdfunding platforms are managed by experienced real estate professionals, ensuring efficient project execution and management.

Disadvantages:

1. **Liquidity Risk**:
   - Real estate investments are generally illiquid, meaning it can be challenging to sell your investment before the project completes. This lack of liquidity can be a significant drawback for investors needing quick access to their funds.

2. **Platform Risk**:
   - The success of your investment is partly dependent on the credibility and stability of the crowdfunding platform. There is a risk of platform failure or fraudulent activities.

3. **Market Risk**:
   - Real estate markets can be volatile. Economic downturns, changes in local market conditions, or project-specific issues can impact the returns on your investment.

4. **Fees**:
   - Crowdfunding platforms often charge fees for their services, which can reduce the net returns for investors. It is essential to understand the fee structure before investing.

How to Get Started with Real Estate Crowdfunding

1. **Research and Select a Platform**:

   - Compare different crowdfunding platforms to find one that suits your investment goals, risk tolerance, and minimum investment requirements. Look for platforms with a good track record, transparent operations, and positive user reviews.

2. **Understand the Investment Options**:

   - Familiarize yourself with the types of investments offered, such as equity vs. debt investments. Review the details of available projects, including projected returns, timelines, and risk factors.

3. **Evaluate the Platform's Due Diligence Process**:

   - Ensure the platform conducts thorough due diligence on listed projects. This includes assessing the developer's experience, project feasibility, market conditions, and financial projections.

4. **Start with Small Investments**:

   - If you are new to real estate crowdfunding, start with small investments to gain experience and understand how the platform operates. This approach allows you to learn without committing significant capital upfront.

5. **Diversify Your Investments**:

   - Spread your investments across multiple projects and platforms to reduce risk. Diversification helps mitigate the impact of underperformance in any single investment.

6. **Monitor Your Investments**:

   - Regularly review the performance of your investments through the platform's dashboard. Stay informed about project developments, income distributions, and any potential issues.

Example Table: Comparing Crowdfunding Platforms

Platform	Minimum Investment	Investment Types	Key Features	Fees
Fundrise	$500	Equity, eREITs	Low minimums, diversified portfolios	0.85% annual fee
RealtyMogul	$1,000	Equity, Debt	Commercial and residential, institutional quality	1% - 1.25% annual fee
CrowdStreet	$25,000	Equity	High-quality commercial projects, accredited only	Variable project fees

Real estate crowdfunding provides an innovative way for individual investors to participate in real estate markets with lower capital requirements and the benefits of professional management. By carefully selecting platforms and projects, diversifying investments, and staying informed about market conditions, investors can build a robust portfolio that generates passive income and potential long-term growth. This approach allows you to leverage the collective power of crowdfunding to achieve your financial goals while managing risk effectively.

Chapter 4: Affiliate Marketing

4.1 Understanding Affiliate Marketing

Affiliate marketing is a popular strategy for generating passive income, leveraging the power of online platforms to promote products or services in exchange for a commission. This section explores what affiliate marketing is, how it works, the key players in the affiliate marketing ecosystem, and the benefits of using affiliate marketing as a source of passive income.

What is Affiliate Marketing and How Does It Work?

Affiliate marketing is a performance-based marketing strategy where an affiliate earns a commission by promoting another company's product or service. The affiliate promotes these products through various channels such as blogs, social media, email newsletters, and websites. Here's a detailed breakdown of how it works:

1. **Joining an Affiliate Program**:

- Affiliates join an affiliate program, often through an affiliate network. Companies offer these programs to incentivize affiliates to promote their products.

- Examples of popular affiliate networks include Amazon Associates, ShareASale, and Commission Junction.

2. **Promoting Products**:

- Affiliates select products or services to promote. They receive a unique affiliate link that tracks the traffic and sales generated from their promotions.

- Promotion methods can vary widely, including writing product reviews, creating how-to guides, or sharing discount codes on social media.

3. **Driving Traffic**:
   - The affiliate's goal is to drive traffic to the merchant's website using their unique affiliate links. This can be achieved through content marketing, paid advertising, SEO, and social media marketing.

4. **Tracking and Sales**:
   - When a consumer clicks on the affiliate link and makes a purchase, the sale is tracked using cookies. These cookies ensure that the affiliate gets credit for the sale even if the consumer doesn't purchase immediately.
   - The merchant processes the transaction, and the affiliate earns a commission based on the sale's value.

5. **Earning Commissions**:
   - Commissions can vary significantly depending on the product and the terms of the affiliate program. Some programs offer a percentage of the sale, while others offer a fixed amount per conversion.

Key Players in the Affiliate Marketing Ecosystem

Understanding the roles of various participants in the affiliate marketing ecosystem is crucial for maximizing its potential. The key players include:

1. **Merchants**:
   - Also known as advertisers or retailers, merchants are the companies that create and sell products or services. They set up affiliate programs to expand their reach and increase sales through affiliate partnerships.
   - Examples include e-commerce sites like Amazon, service providers like Bluehost, and online course platforms like Udemy.

2. **Affiliates**:

- Affiliates, also known as publishers, are individuals or companies that promote the merchant's products in exchange for a commission. They can be bloggers, influencers, content creators, or media companies.

- Successful affiliates typically have a strong online presence and the ability to drive significant traffic to merchant sites.

3. **Affiliate Networks**:

- These platforms act as intermediaries between merchants and affiliates. They provide the infrastructure for tracking sales, managing payments, and offering a marketplace where affiliates can find programs to join.

- Notable affiliate networks include Rakuten, ClickBank, and Impact.

4. **Consumers**:

- Consumers are the end-users who click on affiliate links and make purchases. They drive the affiliate marketing ecosystem by engaging with content created by affiliates and ultimately buying products or services.

- Ensuring a positive experience for consumers is essential for maintaining trust and driving conversions.

Benefits of Affiliate Marketing as a Passive Income Source

Affiliate marketing offers several advantages that make it an attractive option for generating passive income:

1. **Low Startup Costs**:

- Starting with affiliate marketing requires minimal upfront investment. You don't need to create or stock products, handle shipping, or manage customer service. This makes it accessible to anyone with an internet connection and a platform to promote products.

2. **Flexibility and Scalability**:

- Affiliate marketing provides the flexibility to work from anywhere and scale your efforts. You can promote multiple products across different niches and expand your reach over time.

- Successful affiliates can automate many aspects of their business, such as using email marketing tools, content management systems, and social media schedulers to streamline their efforts.

3. **Diverse Income Streams**:

- Affiliates can diversify their income by promoting a range of products and services. This diversification helps mitigate risk if one product's sales decline.

- Commissions can come from a variety of sources, including one-time sales, recurring subscriptions, and performance bonuses.

4. **Performance-Based Earnings**:

- Affiliates earn money based on their performance. This model rewards effective marketing strategies and incentivizes continuous improvement.

- High-performing affiliates can earn significant income by driving large volumes of sales.

5. **Passive Income Potential**:

- Once established, affiliate marketing can generate passive income. Evergreen content, such as blog posts and videos, can continue to drive traffic and sales long after they are created.

- Affiliates can earn money while they sleep, as their promotions work around the clock.

Example Table: Comparison of Popular Affiliate Networks

Network	Commission Structure	Payment Frequency	Minimum Payout	Notable Merchants
Amazon Associates	Percentage of sales	Monthly	$10	Amazon, Audible, Kindle
ShareASale	Fixed and percentage-based	Monthly	$50	Etsy, Reebok, Warby Parker
Commission Junction	Percentage of sales	Monthly	$50	Overstock, GoDaddy, Grammarly
ClickBank	Fixed and percentage-based	Weekly	$10	Health and fitness, digital products

Affiliate marketing is a robust strategy for generating passive income, offering low startup costs, flexibility, and scalability. By understanding the affiliate marketing ecosystem and effectively promoting products, individuals can build a sustainable income stream. With the right approach and consistent effort, affiliate marketing can become a significant component of your passive income strategy.

4.2 Choosing the Right Affiliate Programs

Selecting the right affiliate programs is critical to the success of your affiliate marketing efforts. This involves finding profitable programs, evaluating their suitability, and choosing high-converting products that align with your audience's interests. Here's a comprehensive guide on how to achieve these goals.

How to Find Profitable Affiliate Programs

1. **Research Affiliate Networks**:

   - **Join Reputable Networks**: Start by joining well-known affiliate networks like Amazon Associates, ShareASale, Commission Junction (CJ), and ClickBank. These platforms aggregate numerous affiliate programs across various niches, making it easier to find suitable options.

   - **Explore Specialized Networks**: Depending on your niche, you might also explore specialized affiliate networks such as Impact for influencer marketing or Rakuten Marketing for retail.

2. **Analyze Market Demand**:

   - **Use Keyword Research Tools**: Tools like Google Keyword Planner, Ahrefs, and SEMrush can help identify products with high search volumes, indicating strong market demand.

   - **Trending Products**: Keep an eye on trending products and services in your niche by following industry news, social media trends, and forums like Reddit and Quora.

3. **Competitor Analysis**:

   - **Review Competitor Websites**: Analyze the affiliate programs and products promoted by successful websites in your niche. Tools like SimilarWeb can help identify top-performing affiliate sites and their traffic sources.

   - **Content and Promotion Strategies**: Study how competitors promote affiliate products, including the types of content they create and the marketing channels they use.

Evaluating Affiliate Programs for Suitability

1. **Commission Structure**:

   - **Percentage vs. Fixed Commissions**: Understand whether the program offers a percentage of the sale or a fixed commission per sale. Higher commission rates generally mean better earnings, but consider the average order value as well.

   - **Recurring Commissions**: Some programs offer recurring commissions for subscription-based products, providing ongoing income for as long as the customer remains subscribed.

2. **Cookie Duration**:

   - **Tracking Windows**: Cookie duration determines how long you will receive credit for a sale after a potential customer clicks your affiliate link. Longer cookie durations increase the likelihood of earning commissions.

   - **Industry Standards**: While 30-day cookies are standard, some programs offer 90 days or even lifetime cookies, significantly improving earning potential.

3. **Payout Terms and Thresholds**:

   - **Payment Frequency**: Check how often payments are made (e.g., weekly, monthly). Regular payouts can improve cash flow.

   - **Minimum Payout**: Ensure the minimum payout threshold is achievable. High thresholds can delay receiving your earnings.

4. **Program Reputation and Support**:

   - **Merchant Credibility**: Research the reputation of the merchant and their affiliate program. Look for reviews, ratings, and testimonials from other affiliates.

- **Support and Resources**: A good affiliate program provides support and resources, such as marketing materials, training, and dedicated affiliate managers.

5. **Product Fit and Quality**:

- **Relevance to Audience**: The products should align with your audience's interests and needs. Promoting irrelevant products can damage trust and reduce conversion rates.

- **Product Quality**: Ensure the products are of high quality and provide good value to customers. Positive customer experiences lead to higher conversion rates and repeat sales.

Strategies for Selecting High-Converting Products

1. **Understand Your Audience**:

- **Demographic and Psychographic Analysis**: Know your audience's demographics (age, gender, location) and psychographics (interests, values, pain points). This understanding helps in selecting products that resonate with them.

- **Engagement Metrics**: Use analytics tools to track engagement metrics like page views, time on site, and click-through rates. High engagement indicates interest and can guide product selection.

2. **Focus on Evergreen Products**:

- **Longevity and Demand**: Evergreen products are those with consistent demand over time, such as health supplements, financial tools, and software subscriptions. They provide a steady stream of income.

- **Avoid Fads**: While trending products can provide short-term gains, they often have a limited lifespan. Focus on products with long-term potential.

3. **Leverage Reviews and Case Studies**:

- **User Reviews**: Read user reviews on e-commerce sites and forums to gauge product satisfaction and identify any common issues. High-rated products are more likely to convert.

- **Case Studies and Testimonials**: Case studies and testimonials can provide insights into the product's effectiveness and how it addresses customer needs.

4. **Test and Optimize**:

- **A/B Testing**: Conduct A/B tests on different products and marketing strategies to see what resonates best with your audience. Experiment with different headlines, CTAs, and promotional tactics.

- **Monitor Performance**: Use analytics tools to track conversion rates, click-through rates, and overall sales. Regularly review and adjust your strategies based on performance data.

5. **Utilize Affiliate Tools and Plugins**:

- **Affiliate Link Management**: Tools like ThirstyAffiliates or Pretty Links help manage and cloak your affiliate links, making them more attractive and trustworthy to users.

- **Product Comparison Tables**: Use plugins to create product comparison tables that highlight the features, benefits, and pricing of different products. These can improve user experience and boost conversions.

Example Table: Evaluating Affiliate Programs

Criteria	Amazon Associates	ShareASale	Commission Junction	ClickBank
Commission Structure	Percentage of sales	Fixed and percentage	Percentage of sales	Fixed and percentage
Cookie Duration	24 hours	30-90 days	30 days	60 days
Payout Terms	Monthly	Monthly	Monthly	Weekly
Minimum Payout	$10	$50	$50	$10
Product Range	Extensive	Extensive	Extensive	Digital products

Choosing the right affiliate programs is pivotal for building a successful affiliate marketing business. By conducting thorough research, evaluating programs based on commission structures, cookie durations, and program reputation, and selecting high-converting products that align with your audience's needs, you can optimize your earnings and create a sustainable passive income stream. This strategic approach ensures that your efforts in affiliate marketing are both effective and rewarding.

4.3 Building an Affiliate Marketing Platform

Creating a successful affiliate marketing platform involves developing a robust website or blog, producing high-quality content that drives traffic and conversions, and implementing effective SEO strategies to increase visibility. This section will guide you through these crucial steps to help you build a strong foundation for your affiliate marketing business.

Creating a Website or Blog for Affiliate Marketing

1. **Choose a Niche**:

   - **Focus Area**: Select a niche that you are passionate about and that has a demand for products. A focused niche helps attract a targeted audience, which is more likely to convert.

   - **Research Demand**: Use tools like Google Trends, Keyword Planner, and Ahrefs to identify popular niches and evaluate competition.

2. **Domain and Hosting**:

   - **Domain Name**: Choose a domain name that reflects your niche and is easy to remember. Keep it short, relevant, and avoid using numbers or hyphens.

   - **Hosting Provider**: Select a reliable hosting provider that offers fast load times and minimal downtime. Providers like Bluehost, SiteGround, and WP Engine are popular choices.

3. **Website Design and Setup**:

   - **CMS Platform**: Use a content management system (CMS) like WordPress, which is user-friendly and highly customizable.

   - **Themes and Plugins**: Choose a responsive theme that is visually appealing and optimized for SEO. Install essential plugins for SEO (Yoast SEO), analytics (Google Analytics), and performance (WP Super Cache).

4. **Site Structure**:

   - **User-Friendly Navigation**: Design a clear and intuitive navigation structure. Ensure that your website is easy to navigate, with well-organized categories and a search function.

- **Mobile Optimization**: Ensure your site is mobile-friendly, as a significant portion of traffic comes from mobile devices. Use responsive design techniques to improve user experience on all devices.

Developing Content That Drives Traffic and Conversions

1. **Content Strategy**:

- **Identify Target Audience**: Understand your audience's needs, preferences, and pain points. Create buyer personas to guide your content creation efforts.

- **Content Types**: Develop a variety of content types, including blog posts, reviews, tutorials, comparison guides, and videos. This variety keeps your audience engaged and caters to different learning preferences.

2. **Quality Content Creation**:

- **Informative and Engaging**: Produce high-quality, informative content that provides value to your audience. Use engaging headlines, clear language, and actionable insights.

- **Visual Elements**: Incorporate visuals such as images, infographics, and videos to enhance the content and improve readability. Visuals can also make your content more shareable.

3. **Calls to Action (CTAs)**:

- **Strategic Placement**: Place CTAs strategically within your content to guide readers towards making a purchase or signing up for a newsletter. Ensure they are clear, compelling, and relevant to the content.

- **A/B Testing**: Test different CTA placements, designs, and wording to determine what converts best. Use tools like Google Optimize for A/B testing.

4. **Content Calendar**:

- **Regular Updates**: Maintain a content calendar to plan and schedule regular content updates. Consistency helps build a loyal audience and improves search engine rankings.

- **Seasonal Content**: Incorporate seasonal and trending topics into your content strategy to capture timely interest and boost traffic.

SEO Strategies to Increase Visibility

1. **Keyword Research**:

- **Identify Keywords**: Use keyword research tools to find relevant keywords with high search volume and low competition. Focus on long-tail keywords that are more specific and have a higher conversion rate.

- **Content Optimization**: Integrate target keywords naturally into your content, including titles, headings, meta descriptions, and body text. Avoid keyword stuffing, as it can harm your SEO efforts.

2. **On-Page SEO**:

- **Title Tags and Meta Descriptions**: Write compelling title tags and meta descriptions that include your target keywords. These elements are crucial for search engine rankings and click-through rates.

- **Internal Linking**: Use internal links to connect related content on your site. This helps search engines understand the structure of your site and keeps visitors engaged longer.

- **URL Structure**: Create clean, descriptive URLs that include your target keywords. Avoid using long, complicated URLs.

3. **Technical SEO**:

- **Site Speed**: Optimize your site's loading speed by compressing images, using a content delivery network (CDN), and minimizing code. Fast-loading sites rank higher and provide a better user experience.

- **XML Sitemaps**: Submit an XML sitemap to search engines to ensure all your pages are indexed. Use plugins like Yoast SEO to generate and manage sitemaps.

- **Mobile-Friendliness**: Ensure your site is fully optimized for mobile devices. Google uses mobile-first indexing, so a mobile-friendly site is crucial for SEO.

4. **Off-Page SEO**:

- **Backlink Building**: Build high-quality backlinks from reputable sites to improve your domain authority. Engage in guest blogging, partnerships, and outreach to acquire backlinks.

- **Social Media Promotion**: Promote your content on social media platforms to drive traffic and generate backlinks. Social signals can indirectly influence SEO.

Example Table: SEO Tools Comparison

Tool	Features	Best For	Price
Ahrefs	Keyword research, backlink analysis	Comprehensive SEO analysis	Starts at $99/month
SEMrush	Keyword tracking, site audits	Competitive analysis	Starts at $119.95/month

Tool	Features	Best For	Price
Yoast SEO	On-page optimization, readability	WordPress users	Free, Premium $89/year
Google Analytics	Traffic analysis, user behavior	Website performance tracking	Free
Moz Pro	Keyword research, rank tracking	All-in-one SEO tool	Starts at $99/month

Building a successful affiliate marketing platform requires careful planning, consistent content creation, and effective SEO strategies. By creating a well-structured website or blog, developing high-quality content that attracts and converts visitors, and optimizing your site for search engines, you can establish a strong online presence and generate sustainable passive income through affiliate marketing. This comprehensive approach ensures that your efforts are both efficient and effective, setting the foundation for long-term success.

4.4 Promoting Affiliate Products

Promoting affiliate products effectively is crucial for driving traffic and conversions, which are key to generating passive income through affiliate marketing. This section explores various promotion techniques, tracking and analyzing affiliate performance, and optimizing promotions for higher conversions.

Effective Promotion Techniques

1. **Email Marketing**:

- **Building an Email List**: Start by building a robust email list. Offer incentives like free eBooks, checklists, or exclusive content to encourage sign-ups.

- **Segmenting Your List**: Segment your email list based on interests, demographics, and behavior to send targeted and relevant content. This increases engagement and conversion rates.

- **Crafting Engaging Emails**: Write compelling subject lines and personalized email content. Include strong calls to action (CTAs) and make sure your emails are mobile-friendly.

- **Automating Campaigns**: Use email marketing tools like Mailchimp, AWeber, or ConvertKit to automate your campaigns. Set up automated sequences for new subscribers, product launches, and promotional offers.

2. **Social Media Marketing**:

- **Platform Selection**: Choose the right social media platforms based on where your target audience is most active. Common platforms include Facebook, Instagram, Twitter, and LinkedIn.

- **Content Strategy**: Create a mix of content types, such as posts, stories, videos, and live streams. Share valuable information, engage with your audience, and subtly promote your affiliate products.

- **Influencer Partnerships**: Collaborate with influencers in your niche to reach a wider audience. Influencers can promote your affiliate products through sponsored posts, reviews, and giveaways.

- **Paid Social Advertising**: Utilize paid advertising options on social media to target specific demographics and interests. Platforms like Facebook Ads and Instagram Ads offer powerful targeting tools.

3. **Paid Advertising**:

- **Pay-Per-Click (PPC) Advertising**: Use PPC campaigns on Google Ads and Bing Ads to drive targeted traffic to your affiliate links. Create compelling ad copy and use relevant keywords to reach potential buyers.
- **Display Advertising**: Place banner ads on relevant websites and blogs within your niche. Use eye-catching designs and clear CTAs to attract clicks.
- **Retargeting**: Implement retargeting campaigns to reach users who have previously visited your site but did not convert. Platforms like Google AdWords and Facebook Ads offer retargeting options.

Tracking and Analyzing Affiliate Performance

1. **Setting Up Tracking**:

- **Affiliate Links**: Use unique affiliate links provided by the affiliate program to track clicks and conversions. Tools like Pretty Links and ThirstyAffiliates can help manage and cloak your links.
- **Analytics Tools**: Integrate Google Analytics with your website to track visitor behavior, traffic sources, and conversion paths. Set up goals and events to measure specific actions.

2. **Key Performance Indicators (KPIs)**:

- **Click-Through Rate (CTR)**: Measure the percentage of people who click on your affiliate links compared to the total number of visitors. A higher CTR indicates effective promotions.
- **Conversion Rate**: Track the percentage of visitors who complete a desired action (e.g., making a purchase) after

clicking an affiliate link. A higher conversion rate signifies successful targeting and content.

- **Return on Investment (ROI)**: Calculate the ROI of your marketing efforts by comparing the revenue generated from affiliate commissions to the costs of your promotions.

3. **Regular Reporting and Analysis**:

- **Performance Reports**: Generate regular reports to review the performance of your affiliate marketing campaigns. Analyze trends and identify high-performing strategies.
- **A/B Testing**: Conduct A/B tests on different elements of your campaigns, such as email subject lines, ad copy, and landing page designs. Use the results to optimize your promotions.

Optimizing Promotions for Higher Conversions

1. **Improving Content Quality**:

- **High-Quality Reviews**: Write detailed and honest reviews of affiliate products. Highlight both pros and cons to build trust with your audience.
- **Tutorials and How-Tos**: Create tutorials and how-to guides that demonstrate the use and benefits of the products. Use step-by-step instructions and visuals to enhance understanding.
- **Comparison Articles**: Publish comparison articles that evaluate multiple products in the same category. Help your audience make informed decisions by providing clear comparisons.

2. **Enhancing User Experience**:

- **Fast Loading Pages**: Ensure your website loads quickly to reduce bounce rates and improve user experience. Optimize images and use caching plugins to speed up your site.

- **Mobile Optimization**: Make sure your website is fully responsive and looks great on all devices. Mobile optimization is crucial as many users access content through their smartphones.
- **Clear CTAs**: Use clear and compelling CTAs in your content. Experiment with different placements, colors, and wording to see what drives the most conversions.

3. **Leveraging Social Proof**:

- **Customer Testimonials**: Include testimonials from satisfied customers to build credibility. Real-life experiences can significantly influence purchasing decisions.
- **User-Generated Content**: Encourage your audience to share their experiences with the products you promote. Feature their content on your website and social media channels.
- **Trust Badges and Certifications**: Display trust badges, security seals, and certifications to reassure visitors of the product's reliability and your site's credibility.

Example Table: Tracking and Optimizing Performance Metrics

Metric	Definition	Tool/Method	Optimization Strategy
Click-Through Rate	Percentage of clicks on affiliate links	Google Analytics, Pretty Links	Improve link placement and CTA design
Conversion Rate	Percentage of clicks	Affiliate Dashboard,	Enhance landing pages and

Metric	Definition	Tool/Method	Optimization Strategy
	resulting in sales	Google Analytics	streamline purchase process
Return on Investment	Revenue generated vs. promotion costs	Financial Tracking Software, Excel	Focus on high-performing channels, reduce unnecessary expenses
Bounce Rate	Percentage of visitors leaving quickly	Google Analytics	Improve page load speed, content relevance
Average Order Value	Average amount spent per purchase	Affiliate Dashboard	Promote higher-value products, bundle offers

By effectively promoting affiliate products through targeted email marketing, strategic social media engagement, and efficient paid advertising, you can drive substantial traffic and conversions. Regularly tracking and analyzing performance metrics allows you to refine your strategies and optimize your promotions for higher conversions, ultimately building a sustainable and profitable affiliate marketing business.

4.5 Scaling Your Affiliate Marketing Efforts

Scaling your affiliate marketing efforts involves expanding your reach, leveraging data and analytics for growth, and building strong relationships with affiliate networks. By effectively implementing these strategies, you can significantly increase your revenue and solidify your presence in the affiliate marketing landscape.

Expanding Your Reach with Multiple Platforms

1. **Diversifying Platforms**:

- **Website and Blog**: Ensure your primary platform is well-optimized and regularly updated with high-quality content. Expand by adding niche-specific blogs to target different segments of your audience.

- **Social Media**: Utilize various social media platforms like Facebook, Instagram, Twitter, LinkedIn, and Pinterest to reach broader audiences. Each platform caters to different demographics and can help you tap into diverse market segments.

- **YouTube and Video Content**: Create video content to engage a visual audience. Product reviews, unboxings, tutorials, and comparison videos can drive significant traffic and conversions. Optimize your videos for SEO and include affiliate links in the descriptions.

- **Podcasts**: Launch a podcast to discuss topics relevant to your niche. Promote affiliate products through show notes and episode mentions, reaching an audience that prefers audio content.

2. **Content Syndication**:

- **Guest Blogging**: Write guest posts for other reputable blogs in your niche. This not only expands your reach but also builds backlinks to your site, improving SEO.

- **Content Repurposing**: Repurpose existing content into different formats, such as infographics, eBooks, and slideshows, to reach new audiences and extend the lifespan of your content.

3. **Email Marketing**:

- **Segmented Campaigns**: Create segmented email campaigns to deliver personalized content and product recommendations to different subscriber groups. Tailored emails increase engagement and conversion rates.

- **Lead Magnets**: Use lead magnets like free courses, templates, or exclusive reports to grow your email list. Engage subscribers with valuable content and strategically incorporate affiliate promotions.

Leveraging Data and Analytics for Growth

1. **Tracking Performance Metrics**:

- **Google Analytics**: Use Google Analytics to monitor website traffic, user behavior, and conversion paths. Identify which pages and content types drive the most affiliate sales.

- **Affiliate Dashboards**: Regularly review performance reports from your affiliate programs. Track metrics such as clicks, conversions, and earnings per click (EPC) to evaluate your campaigns.

2. **Data-Driven Decisions**:

- **A/B Testing**: Continuously perform A/B tests on your headlines, CTAs, landing pages, and promotional strategies to determine what works best. Implement changes based on data to optimize performance.

- **Heatmaps and User Behavior Tools**: Tools like Hotjar and Crazy Egg provide insights into how visitors interact with your site. Use this data to improve site navigation, content layout, and overall user experience.

3. **Analyzing Audience Insights**:

- **Demographic Data**: Analyze demographic data to understand who your audience is. Tailor your content and promotions to match their preferences and behaviors.

- **Engagement Metrics**: Track engagement metrics such as time on page, bounce rates, and social shares. High engagement indicates strong interest, which can guide content creation and promotion strategies.

Building Relationships with Affiliate Networks

1. **Active Participation**:

- **Network Forums and Communities**: Join forums and online communities related to your affiliate networks. Participate actively to stay updated on best practices, trends, and new opportunities.

- **Webinars and Events**: Attend webinars, workshops, and conferences hosted by affiliate networks. These events provide valuable learning opportunities and help you connect with other affiliates and industry experts.

2. **Effective Communication**:

- **Affiliate Managers**: Establish a good relationship with your affiliate managers. Regular communication can provide insights into high-converting products, exclusive deals, and custom promotional materials.

- **Feedback and Reporting**: Provide feedback to your affiliate networks about the performance of their products. Share your promotional strategies and results to demonstrate your commitment and professionalism.

3. **Negotiating Better Terms**:

- **Performance-Based Negotiations**: If you consistently drive significant traffic and conversions, leverage your performance to negotiate better commission rates or exclusive deals.

- **Exclusive Partnerships**: Work towards securing exclusive partnerships with top-performing merchants. This can include higher commissions, early access to new products, and dedicated support.

Example Table: Data-Driven Optimization Strategies

Metric	Tool	Optimization Strategy
Website Traffic	Google Analytics	Improve SEO, optimize content for keywords
Conversion Rate	Google Analytics	A/B test CTAs and landing pages
User Behavior	Hotjar, Crazy Egg	Enhance site navigation and user experience
Engagement Metrics	Google Analytics	Create more engaging content, use multimedia
Click-Through Rate	Affiliate Dashboards	Refine promotional tactics and ad placements

Scaling your affiliate marketing efforts requires a strategic approach that includes expanding your reach across multiple platforms, leveraging data and analytics for continuous growth, and building strong relationships with affiliate networks. By diversifying your promotional channels, making data-driven decisions, and fostering productive partnerships, you can significantly enhance your affiliate marketing performance and achieve sustainable long-term success. This comprehensive strategy ensures that your affiliate marketing efforts are not only effective but also scalable, allowing you to maximize your passive income potential.

Chapter 5: E-commerce and Dropshipping

5.1 Introduction to E-commerce

E-commerce has revolutionized the way business is conducted, offering individuals and businesses alike an opportunity to generate passive income with minimal upfront investment and effort. This section provides an overview of e-commerce, explores the differences between traditional e-commerce and dropshipping, and sets realistic expectations for those embarking on this journey.

Overview of E-commerce and Its Potential for Passive Income

E-commerce refers to the buying and selling of goods and services over the internet. This digital marketplace allows entrepreneurs to reach a global audience without the constraints of a physical location. The potential for passive income in e-commerce lies in the ability to automate various aspects of the business, from order processing to customer service.

1. **Global Reach**:

- The internet provides access to a vast customer base, allowing e-commerce businesses to sell products worldwide. This extensive reach can significantly increase sales potential compared to a traditional brick-and-mortar store.

2. **Automation Tools**:

- Numerous tools and platforms are available to automate different parts of an e-commerce business. For example, platforms like Shopify and WooCommerce offer integrated solutions for managing inventory, processing payments, and handling shipping logistics.

3. **Low Overhead Costs**:

- E-commerce businesses typically have lower overhead costs compared to traditional retail. There is no need to rent physical space or hire extensive staff, which reduces initial investment and ongoing expenses.

4. **Scalability**:

- E-commerce businesses can scale more easily than traditional businesses. By leveraging digital marketing strategies and optimizing supply chains, entrepreneurs can expand their operations without significant additional costs.

Differences Between Traditional E-commerce and Dropshipping

While traditional e-commerce and dropshipping share similarities, they differ in several key aspects, particularly in terms of inventory management and fulfillment processes.

1. **Traditional E-commerce**:

- **Inventory Management**: In traditional e-commerce, the business owner purchases products in bulk and stores them in a warehouse or storage facility. They are responsible for managing inventory levels, storing products, and shipping orders directly to customers.

- **Higher Upfront Costs**: This model typically requires a significant upfront investment in inventory and storage space. However, it offers better control over product quality and branding.

- **Order Fulfillment**: The business handles all aspects of order fulfillment, including packaging and shipping. This can be more labor-intensive but allows for a higher degree of customization and control over the customer experience.

2. **Dropshipping**:

- **No Inventory Holding**: In the dropshipping model, the business owner does not hold inventory. Instead, when a customer places an order, the business forwards the order to a third-party supplier, who then ships the product directly to the customer.

- **Lower Upfront Costs**: Dropshipping significantly reduces initial costs as there is no need to purchase inventory upfront. This makes it an attractive option for those with limited capital.

- **Order Fulfillment**: The supplier handles order fulfillment, which reduces the operational burden on the business owner. However, it also means less control over product quality and shipping times.

Setting Realistic Expectations

Entering the e-commerce space with realistic expectations is crucial for long-term success. While e-commerce offers significant potential for passive income, it also requires strategic planning, ongoing effort, and patience.

1. **Initial Setup Effort**:

- **Website Development**: Setting up an e-commerce website requires time and effort. This includes selecting a platform, designing the site, and integrating necessary tools for payment processing, inventory management, and customer support.

- **Product Selection**: Choosing the right products to sell is critical. Conduct market research to identify products with high demand and reasonable competition. Consider factors like product quality, supplier reliability, and profit margins.

2. **Marketing and Traffic Generation**:

- **Digital Marketing**: Effective marketing is essential to drive traffic to your e-commerce site. Utilize various strategies such as search engine optimization (SEO), pay-per-click (PPC) advertising, social media marketing, and email campaigns to attract potential customers.

- **Content Creation**: Creating valuable content, such as blog posts, videos, and tutorials, can help establish your brand, engage your audience, and improve your site's SEO.

3. **Customer Service and Retention**:

- **Customer Support**: Providing excellent customer service is vital for retaining customers and generating repeat sales. Implement support channels such as live chat, email, and phone support to address customer inquiries and issues promptly.

- **Loyalty Programs**: Develop loyalty programs and offer incentives to encourage repeat purchases. Satisfied customers are more likely to become brand advocates and refer new customers to your store.

4. **Continuous Improvement**:

- **Performance Monitoring**: Regularly monitor your site's performance using analytics tools. Track key metrics such as traffic, conversion rates, average order value, and customer acquisition costs to identify areas for improvement.

- **Adaptation and Optimization**: Be prepared to adapt your strategies based on performance data and market trends. Continuously optimize your website, product offerings, and marketing campaigns to stay competitive.

Example Table: Traditional E-commerce vs. Dropshipping

Aspect	Traditional E-commerce	Dropshipping
Inventory Management	Business holds and manages inventory	Supplier holds and manages inventory

Aspect	Traditional E-commerce	Dropshipping
Upfront Costs	Higher due to inventory purchases	Lower due to no inventory purchase
Order Fulfillment	Handled by the business	Handled by the supplier
Control Over Quality	High control over product quality	Limited control over product quality
Scalability	Potentially limited by inventory storage	Highly scalable with low overhead

E-commerce offers a compelling opportunity for generating passive income, with the flexibility to choose between traditional models and dropshipping based on your business goals and resources. By understanding the nuances of each approach, setting realistic expectations, and committing to continuous improvement, you can build a successful e-commerce business that provides sustainable income and growth.

5.2 Setting Up Your E-commerce Store

Launching an e-commerce store is a structured process that requires careful planning and execution. Key steps include choosing the right platform, selecting a niche and identifying target customers, and designing and launching your store. Here's a comprehensive guide to help you set up your e-commerce store professionally and efficiently.

Choosing the Right Platform

1. **Evaluating Popular Platforms**:

Shopify:

- **Ease of Use**: Shopify is user-friendly and requires no coding knowledge, making it ideal for beginners.

- **Features**: It offers a range of features, including integrated payment processing, customizable templates, and extensive app integrations.

- **Support**: Provides 24/7 customer support and a large community of users.

- **Cost**: Subscription-based with plans starting at $29 per month.

WooCommerce:

- **Flexibility**: WooCommerce is a WordPress plugin, offering high customization capabilities for users familiar with WordPress.

- **Features**: Extensive themes and plugins, and the ability to integrate with a wide range of third-party services.

- **Cost**: Free to use, but you'll need to pay for hosting, domain, and additional plugins.

BigCommerce:

- **Scalability**: Ideal for growing businesses that need more advanced features and scalability.

- **Features**: No transaction fees, multi-channel selling capabilities, and robust SEO tools.

- **Cost**: Subscription-based with plans starting at $29.95 per month.

2. **Selecting the Best Fit**:

- **Business Size and Goals**: Consider your current business size and future growth plans. Shopify and BigCommerce are great for scalability, while WooCommerce is perfect for those who want extensive customization.

- **Technical Expertise**: Choose a platform that matches your technical skills. Shopify is more user-friendly for beginners, whereas WooCommerce requires some WordPress knowledge.

- **Budget**: Factor in both the initial setup costs and ongoing expenses. Shopify and BigCommerce have straightforward pricing, while WooCommerce can be more cost-effective but with additional costs for hosting and plugins.

Selecting a Niche and Identifying Target Customers

1. **Choosing a Niche**:

- **Market Research**: Use tools like Google Trends, SEMrush, and Ahrefs to identify popular niches with high demand and low competition.

- **Passion and Expertise**: Select a niche that you are passionate about and have some expertise in. This will help maintain your interest and credibility.

- **Profitability**: Evaluate the profitability of the niche. Consider product pricing, profit margins, and potential for upselling and cross-selling.

2. **Identifying Target Customers**:

- **Demographics**: Determine the age, gender, location, and income level of your target customers. This helps tailor your marketing and product offerings.

- **Psychographics**: Understand the interests, values, and lifestyle of your target audience. This information is crucial for creating relevant content and marketing messages.

- **Customer Pain Points**: Identify the problems or needs of your target customers that your products can solve. Use surveys, interviews, and social media insights to gather this information.

Designing and Launching Your Store

1. **Designing Your Store**:

- **Theme Selection**: Choose a theme that aligns with your brand identity. Shopify and WooCommerce offer a wide range of free and premium themes.

- **User Experience (UX)**: Focus on creating a seamless user experience. Ensure your site is easy to navigate, mobile-friendly, and has fast loading times.

- **Branding**: Incorporate your brand's colors, fonts, and logo into your store's design. Consistent branding helps build trust and recognition.

2. **Setting Up Essential Pages**:

- **Homepage**: Create a compelling homepage that showcases your top products, unique selling propositions (USPs), and key promotions.

- **Product Pages**: Design detailed product pages with high-quality images, descriptions, pricing, and customer reviews. Include clear CTAs to encourage purchases.

- **About Us Page**: Tell your brand's story and highlight what sets you apart from competitors. This helps build a connection with your customers.

- **Contact Page**: Provide multiple contact options, including email, phone, and live chat. Ensure customers can easily reach you for support.

3. **Launching Your Store**:

- **Domain and Hosting**: Secure a domain name that reflects your brand and is easy to remember. Set up reliable hosting if using WooCommerce.

- **Payment Gateways**: Integrate secure payment gateways such as PayPal, Stripe, and credit card processing. Ensure the checkout process is smooth and secure.

- **Shipping and Fulfillment**: Set up shipping options and fulfillment processes. Define shipping rates, delivery times, and return policies.

- **Legal Requirements**: Ensure your store complies with legal requirements, including privacy policies, terms of service, and data protection regulations.

Example Table: Platform Comparison

Feature	Shopify	WooCommerce	BigCommerce
Ease of Use	Very easy	Moderate	Easy
Customization	Moderate	High	Moderate
Cost	From $29/month	Hosting + Plugins	From $29.95/month
Scalability	High	High	Very High
Support	24/7 support	Community support	24/7 support

Setting up an e-commerce store involves careful selection of the right platform, thorough market research to choose a profitable niche and target customers, and meticulous design and launch processes. By following these steps, you can create a professional and effective e-commerce store that lays a strong foundation for generating passive income. With the right strategies and tools, your e-commerce venture can thrive and scale, providing sustainable income and growth opportunities.

5.3 Sourcing Products for Dropshipping

Sourcing reliable products and suppliers is a critical aspect of establishing a successful dropshipping business. This section delves into finding dependable suppliers and products, evaluating product quality and supplier reliability, and setting up dropshipping arrangements effectively.

Finding Reliable Suppliers and Products

1. **Research Suppliers**:

- **Online Marketplaces**: Platforms like AliExpress, Oberlo, and Alibaba are popular for finding dropshipping suppliers. These marketplaces offer a wide range of products and typically include reviews and ratings from other buyers.

- **Dropshipping Directories**: Use directories such as SaleHoo, Worldwide Brands, and Doba. These directories vet suppliers and offer lists of reputable companies, reducing the risk of dealing with unreliable suppliers.

- **Industry Events and Trade Shows**: Attending trade shows and industry events can help you establish direct connections with manufacturers and suppliers. This approach provides an opportunity to see products firsthand and build relationships with suppliers.

2. **Selecting Products**:

- **Market Demand**: Use tools like Google Trends, SEMrush, and Jungle Scout to identify trending products with high demand. Look for products that solve problems, have unique features, or are currently popular in your target market.

- **Profit Margins**: Calculate the potential profit margins for each product. Consider the cost of goods, shipping, and any associated fees. Aim for products with a healthy margin to ensure profitability.
- **Competition Analysis**: Evaluate the competition for each product. High competition can make it challenging to stand out, while low competition might indicate limited demand. Balance these factors to find viable products.

Evaluating Product Quality and Supplier Reliability

1. **Product Quality Assessment**:

- **Sample Orders**: Before committing to a supplier, order samples of the products you intend to sell. This allows you to inspect the quality, packaging, and overall presentation of the product.
- **Customer Reviews**: Read reviews from other buyers to gauge the general sentiment regarding the product's quality. Look for consistent feedback on aspects like durability, functionality, and value for money.
- **Quality Certifications**: Check if the supplier provides any quality certifications or complies with industry standards. Certifications like ISO can indicate a commitment to quality.

2. **Supplier Reliability**:

- **Supplier Reviews and Ratings**: Use platforms that provide ratings and reviews for suppliers. High ratings and positive reviews from other dropshippers are good indicators of reliability.
- **Communication and Responsiveness**: Evaluate the supplier's communication. Reliable suppliers are responsive, transparent, and willing to provide detailed information about their products and services.

- **Order Fulfillment Capability**: Ensure that the supplier can handle your order volume. Discuss lead times, inventory levels, and their ability to scale as your business grows.

Setting Up Dropshipping Arrangements

1. **Negotiating Terms**:

- **Pricing and Discounts**: Negotiate pricing terms with your supplier. Bulk discounts or lower prices for consistent orders can improve your profit margins.

- **Minimum Order Requirements**: Understand any minimum order requirements and negotiate terms that align with your business model, especially if you are starting with lower order volumes.

- **Return Policies**: Establish clear return and refund policies with your supplier. Ensure that these policies are customer-friendly and protect your business from excessive return costs.

2. **Automating the Process**:

- **Integration Tools**: Use dropshipping tools and platforms like Oberlo, Dropified, and Spocket to automate the process of syncing product listings, managing orders, and tracking inventory. These tools streamline operations and reduce manual workload.

- **Order Management**: Set up an efficient order management system. Ensure that orders are automatically forwarded to the supplier and that you can track order status, fulfillment, and shipping updates in real-time.

3. **Legal and Logistical Considerations**:

- **Contracts and Agreements**: Draft formal contracts outlining the terms of your partnership, including pricing, order fulfillment, quality standards, and dispute resolution. This provides legal protection for both parties.

- **Shipping and Delivery**: Work with suppliers to establish reliable shipping methods and timelines. Consider using tracking numbers for all shipments to provide customers with visibility and reduce the risk of lost packages.

- **Customs and Import Regulations**: If you are sourcing products internationally, ensure compliance with customs and import regulations. This includes understanding tariffs, duties, and any required documentation.

Example Table: Supplier Evaluation Criteria

Criteria	Description	Importance
Product Quality	Consistency, durability, and customer satisfaction	High
Supplier Reliability	Communication, responsiveness, and order fulfillment	High
Pricing	Competitive pricing and potential for discounts	Medium
Shipping Efficiency	Speed, reliability, and tracking capabilities	High
Return Policies	Fair and transparent return and refund policies	Medium
Scalability	Ability to handle increased order volumes	High

Finding reliable suppliers and sourcing high-quality products are foundational elements of a successful dropshipping business. By thoroughly evaluating suppliers, assessing product quality, and setting up efficient dropshipping arrangements, you can build a sustainable e-commerce business that delivers value to your customers and generates passive income. This structured approach ensures that your business is well-equipped to handle growth and adapt to market demands, providing a strong foundation for long-term success.

5.4 Marketing Your E-commerce Store

Effectively marketing your e-commerce store is crucial to driving traffic, converting visitors into customers, and building customer loyalty for repeat business. This section outlines strategies for driving traffic using SEO, social media, and PPC, converting visitors into customers, and building a loyal customer base.

Strategies for Driving Traffic to Your Store

1. **Search Engine Optimization (SEO)**:

   - **Keyword Research**: Use tools like Google Keyword Planner, Ahrefs, and SEMrush to identify relevant keywords for your niche. Focus on long-tail keywords that have lower competition and higher conversion potential.

   - **On-Page SEO**: Optimize your product pages, blog posts, and other content by including target keywords in titles, meta descriptions, headers, and body text. Ensure your website is mobile-friendly and has fast loading times.

   - **Content Marketing**: Create high-quality content that addresses your audience's pain points and interests. This can include blog posts, tutorials, product reviews, and buying guides. Consistently publishing valuable content helps improve your search engine rankings and attract organic traffic.

   - **Backlink Building**: Acquire backlinks from reputable websites in your niche. This can be achieved through guest blogging, partnerships, and outreach efforts. High-quality backlinks signal to search engines that your site is authoritative and trustworthy.

2. **Social Media Marketing**:

- **Platform Selection**: Choose the social media platforms where your target audience is most active. Facebook, Instagram, Twitter, and Pinterest are popular choices for e-commerce businesses.

- **Content Strategy**: Develop a content calendar and post regularly. Share a mix of promotional content, user-generated content, behind-the-scenes looks, and educational posts. Use visuals like images and videos to engage your audience.

- **Influencer Marketing**: Partner with influencers in your niche to reach a larger audience. Influencers can create authentic content that promotes your products and drives traffic to your store.

- **Paid Social Advertising**: Utilize paid advertising options on social media platforms. Use advanced targeting options to reach specific demographics and interests. Facebook Ads and Instagram Ads are particularly effective for e-commerce.

3. **Pay-Per-Click (PPC) Advertising**:

- **Google Ads**: Create PPC campaigns using Google Ads to appear in search results for relevant keywords. Focus on high-intent keywords that indicate a readiness to purchase. Use ad extensions to provide additional information and encourage clicks.

- **Remarketing**: Implement remarketing campaigns to target users who have previously visited your site but did not convert. Display ads across various websites to remind them of your products and encourage them to return.

- **Display Advertising**: Use display ads to reach a broader audience. Design eye-catching banners and place them on websites that your target audience frequents.

Converting Visitors into Customers

1. **Optimizing Product Pages**:

   - **High-Quality Images**: Use high-resolution images that show the product from multiple angles. Include zoom functionality and videos to give a comprehensive view.

   - **Compelling Descriptions**: Write detailed and persuasive product descriptions that highlight the benefits and features. Use bullet points for easy readability and include relevant keywords.

   - **Customer Reviews and Ratings**: Display customer reviews and ratings on product pages. Positive reviews build trust and can significantly impact purchasing decisions.

2. **Streamlining the Checkout Process**:

   - **Simplified Checkout**: Minimize the steps required to complete a purchase. Offer guest checkout options and avoid asking for unnecessary information.

   - **Multiple Payment Options**: Provide various payment methods, including credit/debit cards, PayPal, and other digital wallets. This ensures convenience for a wider range of customers.

   - **Security and Trust Signals**: Display security badges and SSL certificates to reassure customers that their payment information is safe. Trust signals like money-back guarantees and easy return policies also help increase conversions.

3. **Personalization and Upselling**:

   - **Personalized Recommendations**: Use customer data to provide personalized product recommendations based on browsing and purchase history. Personalized experiences can increase engagement and sales.

- **Upselling and Cross-Selling**: Suggest complementary products or higher-end versions of the product being viewed. Use phrases like "Customers also bought" or "You might also like" to introduce these options.

Building Customer Loyalty and Repeat Business

1. **Exceptional Customer Service**:

- **Responsive Support**: Provide multiple channels for customer support, including live chat, email, and phone. Ensure timely and helpful responses to customer inquiries and issues.

- **Post-Purchase Engagement**: Follow up with customers after their purchase. Send thank-you emails, ask for feedback, and offer support for any issues they might face.

2. **Loyalty Programs**:

- **Reward Systems**: Implement a loyalty program that rewards customers for repeat purchases, referrals, and other engagement activities. Offer points that can be redeemed for discounts, free products, or exclusive offers.

- **Exclusive Offers**: Provide exclusive deals and early access to new products for loyalty program members. This makes them feel valued and encourages repeat business.

3. **Email Marketing**:

- **Regular Newsletters**: Send regular newsletters to keep your audience informed about new products, promotions, and industry news. Ensure the content is valuable and relevant to maintain engagement.

- **Automated Campaigns**: Set up automated email campaigns for abandoned cart reminders, re-engagement of inactive customers, and personalized product recommendations.

Example Table: Marketing Strategies Comparison

Strategy	Benefits	Challenges	Tools/Platforms
SEO	Long-term traffic, cost-effective	Time-consuming, requires expertise	Google Analytics, Ahrefs, SEMrush
Social Media	Direct engagement, brand building	Algorithm changes, content consistency	Facebook, Instagram, Hootsuite
PPC	Immediate traffic, targeted advertising	Costly, requires constant optimization	Google Ads, Bing Ads, Facebook Ads
Email Marketing	High ROI, direct communication	List management, content relevance	Mailchimp, AWeber, ConvertKit

Effectively marketing your e-commerce store involves a mix of SEO, social media, and PPC strategies to drive traffic, coupled with conversion optimization techniques to turn visitors into customers. Building customer loyalty through exceptional service, loyalty programs, and email marketing ensures repeat business and sustainable growth. By implementing these strategies, you can create a thriving e-commerce store that continuously attracts, converts, and retains customers.

5.5 Automating Your E-commerce Business

Automation is a powerful strategy for managing an e-commerce business efficiently while minimizing workload. This section explores the tools and software for automating store operations, the benefits of outsourcing tasks to virtual assistants, and strategies for scaling your business while maintaining a lean operation.

Tools and Software for Automating Store Operations

1. **Inventory Management**:

- **TradeGecko**: Helps automate inventory tracking, order management, and sales forecasting. Integrates with various e-commerce platforms and provides real-time inventory updates.

- **Ordoro**: Automates dropshipping, inventory management, and shipping processes. It supports bulk printing of shipping labels and integrates with multiple sales channels.

2. **Order Processing**:

- **ShipStation**: Streamlines order processing and shipping. It integrates with e-commerce platforms and marketplaces, providing automation for shipping labels, tracking, and returns management.

- **AfterShip**: Automates shipment tracking and sends notifications to customers. It helps reduce the workload associated with tracking multiple shipments and keeps customers informed.

3. **Customer Relationship Management (CRM)**:

- **HubSpot CRM**: Manages customer interactions and stores customer data. Automates email marketing campaigns and tracks customer engagement.

- **Salesforce**: A comprehensive CRM tool that automates sales, customer service, and marketing processes. It offers advanced analytics and reporting features.

4. **Marketing Automation**:

- **Mailchimp**: Automates email marketing campaigns, including welcome emails, abandoned cart reminders, and product recommendations. It also provides analytics to track campaign performance.

- **Hootsuite**: Schedules and manages social media posts across multiple platforms. Automates social media marketing efforts and provides insights into engagement metrics.

5. **E-commerce Platform Automation**:

- **Shopify**: Offers built-in automation tools like Shopify Flow, which automates repetitive tasks such as inventory updates, order tracking, and customer segmentation.

- **WooCommerce**: Integrates with various plugins like WooCommerce Subscriptions and WooCommerce Bookings to automate recurring payments and appointment scheduling.

Outsourcing Tasks to Virtual Assistants

1. **Identifying Tasks for Outsourcing**:

- **Administrative Tasks**: Routine tasks such as email management, data entry, and calendar scheduling can be outsourced to virtual assistants (VAs) to free up your time.

- **Customer Service**: VAs can handle customer inquiries, process returns, and manage live chat support, ensuring consistent and timely responses.

- **Content Creation**: Outsource tasks like blog writing, social media posting, and graphic design to specialized VAs to maintain a consistent content strategy.

2. **Finding and Hiring Virtual Assistants**:

- **Freelance Platforms**: Use platforms like Upwork, Fiverr, and Freelancer to find qualified VAs. These platforms provide access to a global talent pool and offer various skill levels.

- **VA Agencies**: Consider hiring through virtual assistant agencies that provide pre-vetted and trained VAs. Agencies like Belay, Time Etc, and Zirtual offer reliable services and ongoing support.

- **Interview and Onboarding**: Conduct thorough interviews to assess skills and compatibility. Provide clear instructions, training materials, and ongoing feedback to ensure a smooth onboarding process.

3. **Managing Virtual Assistants**:

- **Communication Tools**: Use tools like Slack, Zoom, and Microsoft Teams to maintain regular communication with your VAs. Schedule weekly check-ins and use project management tools like Trello or Asana to track progress.

- **Performance Tracking**: Set clear performance metrics and goals. Use time-tracking software like Time Doctor or Hubstaff to monitor productivity and ensure tasks are completed on time.

Scaling Your Business While Minimizing Workload

1. **Expanding Product Lines**:

- **Market Research**: Use analytics tools to identify best-selling products and customer preferences. Expand your product lines based on demand and trends.

- **Supplier Relationships**: Build strong relationships with reliable suppliers to ensure a steady supply of products. Negotiate favorable terms and bulk discounts to improve margins.

2. **Enhancing Marketing Efforts**:

- **Data-Driven Marketing**: Utilize data analytics to refine your marketing strategies. Identify high-performing channels and allocate your budget accordingly.

- **Automated Campaigns**: Implement automated marketing campaigns for product launches, seasonal promotions, and customer re-engagement. Tools like Klaviyo and ActiveCampaign can help personalize and automate these efforts.

3. **Optimizing Operations**:

- **Standard Operating Procedures (SOPs)**: Develop detailed SOPs for all business processes. This ensures consistency and efficiency, making it easier to delegate tasks and onboard new team members.

- **Technology Integration**: Integrate various tools and software to create a seamless workflow. Use APIs and automation tools like Zapier to connect different systems and automate data transfers.

4. **Leveraging Analytics for Growth**:

- **Sales Analytics**: Use tools like Google Analytics, Shopify Analytics, and WooCommerce Analytics to track sales performance, customer behavior, and conversion rates. Identify areas for improvement and growth opportunities.

- **Customer Insights**: Analyze customer data to understand purchasing patterns, preferences, and lifetime value. Tailor your marketing and product strategies to meet their needs and increase customer retention.

Example Table: Automation Tools Comparison

Tool	Function	Key Features	Cost
TradeGecko	Inventory Management	Real-time tracking, sales forecasting	Starts at $39/month
ShipStation	Order Processing	Shipping labels, tracking, returns	Starts at $9/month
HubSpot CRM	Customer Relationship Mgmt	Email automation, customer tracking	Free, paid plans available
Mailchimp	Marketing Automation	Email campaigns, analytics	Free, paid plans available
Hootsuite	Social Media Management	Scheduling, analytics	Starts at $19/month
Upwork	Hiring Virtual Assistants	Global talent pool, various skills	Project-based fees
Slack	Communication	Messaging, file sharing, integrations	Free, paid plans available

By implementing automation tools and outsourcing tasks to virtual assistants, you can significantly reduce the workload involved in running your e-commerce business. This allows you to focus on strategic growth initiatives and scale your business efficiently. Utilizing data and analytics further enhances your ability to make informed decisions, optimize operations, and drive long-term success.

Chapter 6: Blogging for Passive Income

6.1 Starting a Blog

Creating a successful blog involves several crucial steps, including choosing a profitable niche, setting up your blog with the right domain, hosting, and design, and developing a comprehensive content plan. This section will guide you through these steps to help you establish a strong foundation for your blogging journey.

Choosing a Profitable Niche

1. **Identify Your Interests and Expertise**:

   - **Passion and Knowledge**: Choose a niche that aligns with your interests and expertise. Writing about something you are passionate about will help you stay motivated and produce high-quality content.
   - **Sustainable Interest**: Ensure that your chosen niche is something you can sustain interest in for the long term. Consistency is key to building a successful blog.

2. **Market Research**:

   - **Audience Demand**: Use tools like Google Trends, SEMrush, and Ahrefs to research the popularity and search volume of potential niches. Identify topics that have a high demand but manageable competition.
   - **Monetization Potential**: Consider the monetization potential of your niche. Look for niches with multiple revenue streams, such as affiliate marketing, sponsored posts, digital products, and ad revenue.

3. **Competitive Analysis**:

- **Competitor Blogs**: Analyze successful blogs in your chosen niche. Identify their strengths and weaknesses, content strategies, and engagement levels. This will help you understand what works and find gaps you can fill.

- **Unique Selling Proposition (USP)**: Define your USP to differentiate your blog from competitors. Determine what unique value you can offer to your audience that others do not.

Setting Up Your Blog (Domain, Hosting, Design)

1. **Choosing a Domain Name**:

- **Relevance and Simplicity**: Select a domain name that reflects your niche and is easy to remember. Keep it short, relevant, and avoid using numbers or hyphens.

- **Domain Extensions**: Opt for a .com extension if possible, as it is the most recognized and trusted by users. However, other extensions like .net or .org can also be considered if the .com is unavailable.

2. **Selecting a Hosting Provider**:

- **Reliable Hosting**: Choose a reputable hosting provider that offers reliable uptime, fast load times, and excellent customer support. Popular options include Bluehost, SiteGround, and HostGator.

- **Scalability**: Ensure the hosting provider can accommodate your blog's growth. Look for flexible plans that allow you to upgrade as your traffic increases.

3. **Setting Up Your Blog**:

- **WordPress Installation**: WordPress is the most popular blogging platform due to its flexibility and user-friendly interface. Most hosting providers offer one-click WordPress installation.

- **Choosing a Theme**: Select a responsive and customizable theme that suits your niche and brand identity. Free and premium themes are available on platforms like ThemeForest and the WordPress theme repository.

- **Essential Plugins**: Install essential plugins to enhance your blog's functionality. Key plugins include Yoast SEO for search engine optimization, Akismet for spam protection, and Jetpack for performance and security.

4. **Design and User Experience (UX)**:

- **Clean and Intuitive Design**: Ensure your blog has a clean, intuitive design that makes navigation easy for users. Use a consistent color scheme and readable fonts.

- **Mobile Optimization**: Make sure your blog is mobile-friendly. A significant portion of web traffic comes from mobile devices, so your site must be optimized for all screen sizes.

- **Site Structure**: Organize your content with clear categories and tags. This helps users find relevant content easily and improves your site's SEO.

Creating a Content Plan

1. **Content Strategy**:

- **Defining Your Goals**: Establish clear goals for your blog, such as increasing traffic, generating leads, or building a community. Your content strategy should align with these goals.

- **Audience Persona**: Create detailed audience personas to understand who your readers are, their pain points, and what type of content they find valuable.

2. **Content Types and Formats**:

- **Blog Posts**: Write informative and engaging blog posts that address your audience's needs. Use a mix of listicles, how-to guides, opinion pieces, and case studies to keep your content diverse.

- **Multimedia Content**: Incorporate multimedia elements like images, infographics, and videos to make your content more engaging and shareable.

3. **Editorial Calendar**:

- **Regular Posting Schedule**: Develop an editorial calendar to plan and schedule your content. Consistent posting helps build and retain your audience.

- **Content Ideas**: Brainstorm and list content ideas in advance. Use tools like BuzzSumo to identify trending topics and popular content in your niche.

4. **SEO Optimization**:

- **Keyword Research**: Conduct thorough keyword research to identify relevant keywords for your content. Use these keywords naturally throughout your posts to improve search engine rankings.

- **On-Page SEO**: Optimize each post for on-page SEO by including keywords in the title, headers, meta descriptions, and alt tags for images.

- **Internal Linking**: Link to other relevant posts on your blog to improve navigation and keep readers engaged. This also helps with SEO by creating a robust internal link structure.

5. **Promoting Your Content**:

- **Social Media**: Share your blog posts on social media platforms to drive traffic and increase visibility. Engage with your audience by responding to comments and participating in relevant discussions.

- **Email Marketing**: Build an email list and send regular newsletters with your latest content, special offers, and updates. This helps keep your audience engaged and encourages repeat visits to your blog.

- **Guest Posting**: Write guest posts for other blogs in your niche to reach a wider audience and build backlinks to your site. This can improve your blog's SEO and drive more traffic.

Example Table: Blogging Platform Comparison

Feature	WordPress.org	Blogger	Wix	Squarespace
Ease of Use	Moderate	Easy	Easy	Easy
Customization	High	Limited	Moderate	Moderate
Cost	Hosting + Domain	Free	Subscription	Subscription
Plugins/Add-ons	Extensive	Limited	Limited	Limited

Feature	WordPress.org	Blogger	Wix	Squarespace
Support	Community Support	Limited	Customer Support	Customer Support

Starting a blog involves careful planning and execution, from choosing a profitable niche to setting up your blog with the right domain, hosting, and design, and creating a comprehensive content plan. By following these steps, you can establish a strong foundation for your blog, attract a dedicated audience, and build a sustainable source of passive income. With consistent effort and strategic planning, your blog can become a successful and rewarding venture.

6.2 Creating High-Quality Content

Creating high-quality content is essential for attracting and retaining readers, building your blog's reputation, and improving your search engine rankings. This section covers the key aspects of writing engaging and valuable blog posts, using multimedia to enhance content, and implementing SEO best practices for bloggers.

Writing Engaging and Valuable Blog Posts

1. **Understanding Your Audience**:

- **Audience Research**: Know your audience's demographics, interests, pain points, and preferences. Use surveys, social media insights, and analytics tools to gather this information.

- **Tailored Content**: Create content that addresses your audience's specific needs and questions. This relevance will increase engagement and reader satisfaction.

2. **Crafting Compelling Headlines**:

- **Attention-Grabbing**: Write headlines that capture attention and encourage clicks. Use numbers, power words, and clear benefits to make your headlines stand out.

- **SEO Optimization**: Include relevant keywords in your headlines to improve search engine visibility. Ensure they accurately reflect the content of the post.

3. **Writing Style and Structure**:

- **Clarity and Conciseness**: Write in a clear, concise manner. Avoid jargon and complex language unless your audience is familiar with it.

- **Engaging Introduction**: Start with a compelling introduction that hooks readers and clearly states what they will learn or gain from the post.

- **Readable Formatting**: Use short paragraphs, bullet points, subheadings, and whitespace to make your content easy to read. This improves user experience and keeps readers engaged.

4. **Depth and Value**:

- **In-Depth Analysis**: Provide thorough and well-researched content. Back up your points with data, statistics, and credible sources.

- **Actionable Insights**: Offer practical advice and actionable steps. Readers should feel they have gained something useful that they can apply.

5. **Call to Action (CTA)**:

- **Clear and Relevant**: End your posts with a clear call to action, whether it's to leave a comment, share the post, subscribe to your newsletter, or explore related content.

- **Encourage Engagement**: Ask questions or invite readers to share their experiences in the comments. This fosters community and interaction on your blog.

Using Multimedia to Enhance Content

1. **Incorporating Images**:

- **Visual Appeal**: Use high-quality images to break up text and make your posts more visually appealing. Images can illustrate points, show examples, and add interest.

- **Optimization**: Optimize images for web use by compressing them to reduce file size without compromising quality. Use descriptive file names and alt text for SEO benefits.

2. **Adding Videos**:

- **Engagement**: Videos can significantly increase engagement. Use videos to explain complex topics, demonstrate products, or share interviews and tutorials.

- **Integration**: Embed videos directly into your blog posts from platforms like YouTube or Vimeo. Ensure they are relevant to the content and enhance the reader's understanding.

3. **Infographics and Charts**:

- **Data Visualization**: Infographics and charts are excellent for presenting data in an easy-to-understand format. They can summarize information and highlight key points effectively.

- **Creation Tools**: Use tools like Canva, Piktochart, or Adobe Spark to create professional-looking infographics. Ensure they are branded consistently with your blog's style.

4. **Interactive Elements**:

- **Quizzes and Polls**: Incorporate interactive elements like quizzes and polls to engage readers and encourage participation. These can provide insights into your audience's preferences and opinions.

- **Downloadable Resources**: Offer downloadable resources like eBooks, checklists, and templates. These add value and can help build your email list.

SEO Best Practices for Bloggers

1. **Keyword Research**:

- **Identifying Keywords**: Use tools like Google Keyword Planner, Ahrefs, and SEMrush to find keywords relevant to your niche. Focus on long-tail keywords that have lower competition and higher intent.

- **Strategic Placement**: Incorporate keywords naturally throughout your post, including in the title, headings, meta descriptions, and body text. Avoid keyword stuffing, which can negatively impact SEO.

2. **On-Page SEO**:

- **Title Tags and Meta Descriptions**: Write unique and compelling title tags and meta descriptions for each post. These should include your main keywords and accurately describe the content.

- **Header Tags**: Use header tags (H1, H2, H3) to structure your content. This makes it easier for search engines to understand the hierarchy and relevance of your content.

- **Internal and External Links**: Include internal links to other relevant posts on your blog to improve navigation and SEO. Also, link to credible external sources to back up your points and provide additional value to readers.

3. **Technical SEO**:

- **Site Speed**: Ensure your blog loads quickly. Use tools like Google PageSpeed Insights to identify and fix issues that may be slowing down your site.

- **Mobile Optimization**: Make sure your blog is fully responsive and provides a great user experience on all devices. Google prioritizes mobile-friendly sites in its rankings.

- **XML Sitemaps**: Create and submit an XML sitemap to search engines to help them index your blog more efficiently. Use plugins like Yoast SEO to generate and manage your sitemap.

4. **Content Updates and Refreshes**:

- **Regular Updates**: Regularly update your content to keep it relevant and accurate. This can improve your rankings and provide a better experience for readers.

- **Historical Optimization**: Re-optimize older posts that still attract traffic. Update keywords, add new information, and enhance multimedia elements to keep the content fresh.

Example Table: SEO Best Practices Checklist

SEO Element	Action	Tool/Method
Keyword Research	Identify relevant keywords	Google Keyword Planner, Ahrefs, SEMrush
Title Tags	Include main keyword, keep it under 60 characters	Yoast SEO, manual writing
Meta Descriptions	Write compelling descriptions with keywords	Yoast SEO, manual writing
Header Tags	Use H1 for titles, H2/H3 for subheadings	WordPress editor, HTML coding
Image Optimization	Compress images, use descriptive alt text	TinyPNG, ShortPixel, manual alt text
Internal Linking	Link to related posts within your blog	WordPress editor, SEO plugins
Site Speed	Optimize images, leverage browser caching	Google PageSpeed Insights, GTmetrix
Mobile Optimization	Ensure responsive design, test on multiple devices	Responsive design themes, Google Mobile-Friendly Test

Creating high-quality content that is engaging, valuable, and optimized for search engines is essential for building a successful blog. By understanding your audience, using multimedia elements effectively, and following SEO best practices, you can attract and retain readers, improve your blog's visibility, and establish a strong online presence. With consistent effort and strategic planning, your blog can become a valuable asset that generates passive income and grows over time.

6.3 Monetizing Your Blog

Monetizing your blog involves implementing various strategies to generate revenue from your content and traffic. This section explores affiliate marketing for bloggers, display advertising, and sponsored posts and partnerships to help you build a sustainable income stream.

Affiliate Marketing for Bloggers

1. **Choosing the Right Affiliate Programs**:

   - **Relevance to Your Niche**: Select affiliate programs that are closely related to your blog's niche and audience. Promoting products that your readers are genuinely interested in increases the likelihood of conversions.

   - **High-Quality Products**: Partner with reputable companies that offer high-quality products or services. This ensures that you maintain trust with your audience.

   - **Commission Rates**: Compare commission rates among different programs. Higher rates can significantly boost your earnings, but also consider the average order value and conversion rates.

2. **Integrating Affiliate Links**:

- **Contextual Placement**: Place affiliate links naturally within your content. For example, if you're writing a product review, include links to where readers can purchase the product.

- **Disclosure**: Be transparent with your audience about your affiliate relationships. Include a disclosure statement to comply with legal requirements and build trust with your readers.

- **Resource Pages**: Create dedicated pages for affiliate products, such as a "Resources" or "Recommended Tools" page, where you list and link to products you use and recommend.

3. **Optimizing Affiliate Marketing**:

- **Product Reviews and Tutorials**: Write detailed reviews and tutorials that highlight the benefits and features of the products you're promoting. Use personal anecdotes and examples to make your content relatable.

- **Email Marketing**: Use email newsletters to promote affiliate products. Segment your email list to send targeted recommendations to different audience groups.

- **Analytics and Tracking**: Monitor the performance of your affiliate links using tools like Google Analytics and the affiliate program's dashboard. Track clicks, conversions, and earnings to optimize your strategy.

Display Advertising (Google AdSense, Media.net)

1. **Setting Up Display Ads**:

- **Google AdSense**: Sign up for Google AdSense, which matches ads to your site based on your content and audience. Once approved, you can place ad units on your blog, and you'll earn money when visitors view or click on the ads.

- **Media.net**: Another popular option is Media.net, which offers contextual ads powered by Yahoo and Bing. Similar to AdSense, it provides high-quality ads that match your content.

2. **Ad Placement and Optimization**:

- **Strategic Placement**: Place ads in high-visibility areas of your blog, such as the header, sidebar, and within the content. However, balance ad placement to avoid overwhelming your readers.

- **Ad Formats**: Experiment with different ad formats, such as display ads, text ads, and native ads. Test which formats perform best with your audience.

- **Performance Monitoring**: Regularly review the performance of your ads using the analytics provided by AdSense or Media.net. Adjust placements and formats based on the data to maximize your earnings.

3. **Maximizing Ad Revenue**:

- **Traffic Growth**: Focus on increasing your blog's traffic, as higher traffic levels generally lead to higher ad revenue. Implement SEO strategies, promote your content on social media, and engage with your audience to drive more visitors to your site.

- **Content Quality**: Maintain high-quality content to keep visitors engaged and reduce bounce rates. Engaged readers are more likely to interact with ads.

- **Ad Density**: Avoid placing too many ads on your blog, as this can lead to a poor user experience and potentially violate ad network policies. Find a balance that maximizes revenue without compromising user satisfaction.

Sponsored Posts and Partnerships

1. **Finding Sponsored Opportunities**:

- **Reach Out to Brands**: Proactively contact brands that align with your blog's niche. Pitch collaboration ideas, such as sponsored posts, product reviews, or social media campaigns.

- **Influencer Networks**: Join influencer marketing platforms like AspireIQ, Influence.co, and TapInfluence to connect with brands looking for bloggers to collaborate with.

- **Media Kits**: Create a professional media kit that includes information about your blog, audience demographics, traffic statistics, and previous collaborations. This helps brands understand your value and reach.

2. **Creating Sponsored Content**:

- **Authenticity**: Ensure that sponsored content aligns with your blog's voice and values. Write genuine and honest posts that provide value to your readers while meeting the brand's objectives.

- **Clear Disclosure**: Clearly disclose sponsored content to maintain transparency and comply with legal requirements. Use phrases like "This post is sponsored by [Brand]" at the beginning of the post.

- **Engaging Formats**: Use various content formats, such as blog posts, videos, and social media posts, to create engaging and versatile sponsored content.

3. **Negotiating and Managing Partnerships**:

- **Fair Compensation**: Negotiate fair compensation for your work based on the scope of the collaboration, your blog's reach, and the value you provide. Consider offering different package options for brands to choose from.

- **Contracts**: Use contracts to formalize agreements with brands. Include details about deliverables, timelines, payment terms, and disclosure requirements.

- **Performance Reporting**: Provide brands with performance reports after the collaboration. Include metrics such as page views, engagement rates, and social media reach to demonstrate the value of the partnership.

Example Table: Monetization Methods Comparison

Method	Pros	Cons	Potential Earnings
Affiliate Marketing	High earning potential, relevant to content	Requires ongoing content creation and promotion	Varies widely, can be high
Display Advertising	Passive income, easy to implement	Dependent on traffic volume, can affect UX	Moderate, depends on traffic
Sponsored Posts	High earning potential, builds brand relationships	Requires negotiation and content creation	High, depending on the brand

Monetizing your blog through affiliate marketing, display advertising, and sponsored posts offers multiple revenue streams and helps build a sustainable income. By carefully selecting and integrating these methods, optimizing their performance, and maintaining transparency with your audience, you can effectively monetize your blog while providing value to your readers. This strategic approach ensures long-term success and profitability in your blogging venture.

6.4 Building and Engaging Your Audience

Building a loyal and engaged audience is critical to the success of your blog. This section covers strategies for growing your blog audience, engaging with readers through comments and social media, and building an email list for marketing.

Strategies for Growing Your Blog Audience

1. **Content Quality and Consistency**:

    - **High-Quality Content**: Ensure your content is informative, valuable, and well-written. High-quality content attracts readers and encourages them to share your posts.

    - **Consistent Posting Schedule**: Establish a consistent posting schedule. Regular updates keep your audience engaged and coming back for more. Use an editorial calendar to plan and organize your content.

2. **Search Engine Optimization (SEO)**:

    - **Keyword Research**: Conduct thorough keyword research to identify terms and phrases your target audience is searching for. Incorporate these keywords naturally into your content.

- **On-Page SEO**: Optimize your posts for SEO by using relevant keywords in titles, headings, meta descriptions, and alt text for images. Ensure your site is mobile-friendly and has fast loading times.

- **Backlink Building**: Increase your blog's authority by acquiring backlinks from reputable sites. Guest posting, influencer outreach, and content partnerships can help you build a strong backlink profile.

3. **Social Media Promotion**:

- **Platform Selection**: Choose the social media platforms where your target audience is most active. Focus your efforts on 2-3 platforms to start, such as Facebook, Instagram, and Twitter.

- **Content Sharing**: Share your blog posts on social media with compelling captions and visuals. Use relevant hashtags to increase visibility and reach a broader audience.

- **Engagement**: Engage with your social media followers by responding to comments, participating in discussions, and sharing user-generated content. Building a community around your blog helps foster loyalty.

4. **Collaborations and Guest Blogging**:

- **Guest Posts**: Write guest posts for other popular blogs in your niche. This exposes your content to a new audience and drives traffic back to your site.

- **Collaborations**: Partner with other bloggers and influencers for joint ventures, such as webinars, giveaways, or co-authored content. Collaborations can significantly expand your reach.

Engaging with Readers Through Comments and Social Media

1. **Encouraging Comments**:

   - **Call to Action**: End your posts with questions or prompts that encourage readers to leave comments. For example, ask for their opinions, experiences, or suggestions related to the topic.

   - **Replying to Comments**: Respond to comments promptly and thoughtfully. Engaging with your readers shows that you value their input and fosters a sense of community.

2. **Social Media Interaction**:

   - **Active Presence**: Maintain an active presence on your chosen social media platforms. Post regularly, share updates, and engage with your followers by liking, commenting, and sharing their content.

   - **Live Sessions**: Host live Q&A sessions, webinars, or live streams to interact with your audience in real-time. This helps build a stronger connection and allows you to address their questions and concerns directly.

3. **Community Building**:

   - **Online Communities**: Create online communities, such as Facebook groups or forums, where readers can interact with you and each other. This encourages ongoing engagement and loyalty.

   - **Content Polls and Surveys**: Use polls and surveys to gather feedback and involve your audience in content decisions. This makes them feel valued and more invested in your blog.

Building an Email List for Marketing

1. **Email Capture Techniques**:

   - **Lead Magnets**: Offer valuable lead magnets, such as eBooks, checklists, templates, or exclusive content, in exchange for email sign-ups. Ensure the lead magnet is relevant and useful to your audience.

   - **Opt-In Forms**: Place opt-in forms strategically on your blog, such as at the end of posts, in the sidebar, or as a pop-up. Use clear and compelling calls to action to encourage sign-ups.

2. **Email Marketing Strategy**:

   - **Regular Newsletters**: Send regular newsletters to keep your audience informed about new content, updates, and special offers. Consistency is key to maintaining engagement.

   - **Personalization**: Personalize your emails by addressing subscribers by their name and tailoring content to their interests. Segmentation can help you send more targeted and relevant emails.

   - **Automation**: Use email marketing tools like Mailchimp, ConvertKit, or AWeber to automate your email campaigns. Set up welcome sequences, drip campaigns, and re-engagement emails to nurture your subscribers.

3. **Content and Offers**:

   - **Valuable Content**: Provide valuable content in your emails, such as exclusive insights, tips, and resources. Ensure that your emails offer something of value to your subscribers.

- **Promotions and Discounts**: Use your email list to promote products, services, or special offers. Exclusive discounts and early access to new content can incentivize subscribers to stay engaged.

Example Table: Email Marketing Tools Comparison

Tool	Features	Pricing	Best For
Mailchimp	Automation, templates, analytics	Free, Paid plans start at $9.99/month	Beginners, small businesses
ConvertKit	Automation, landing pages, segmentation	Free, Paid plans start at $29/month	Bloggers, content creators
AWeber	Automation, templates, split testing	Free, Paid plans start at $19/month	Small to medium businesses
GetResponse	Automation, landing pages, webinars	Free, Paid plans start at $15/month	E-commerce, marketers

Building and engaging your audience requires a strategic approach that combines high-quality content, effective promotion, and active interaction with readers. By implementing these strategies, you can grow a loyal audience that regularly engages with your blog and supports its growth. Additionally, building an email list provides a direct channel to communicate with your audience, fostering deeper connections and driving long-term success.

6.5 Scaling Your Blogging Income

Scaling your blogging income involves diversifying revenue streams, collaborating with other bloggers and influencers, and continuously optimizing and updating your content. These strategies can help you increase earnings, expand your reach, and maintain sustainable growth.

Diversifying Income Streams

1. **Digital Products**:

- **eBooks**: Create and sell eBooks that provide in-depth information on topics related to your blog. Use your expertise to offer valuable insights, tips, and solutions that your audience seeks.

- **Templates and Printables**: Design templates, planners, or printables that your readers can use. These products are often highly sought after for their practicality and ease of use.

- **Software and Tools**: If you have technical skills, consider developing software or tools that solve specific problems for your audience. These can range from simple calculators to more complex applications.

2. **Online Courses**:

- **Course Creation**: Develop comprehensive online courses that teach your audience valuable skills. Platforms like Teachable, Udemy, and Kajabi provide the tools to create, host, and sell your courses.

- **Webinars and Workshops**: Host live webinars and workshops to engage with your audience in real-time. This interactive format allows for immediate feedback and higher perceived value.

- **Membership Sites**: Create a membership site where subscribers pay a recurring fee for access to exclusive content, courses, and community support. This model provides a steady income stream and fosters a loyal community.

3. **Memberships and Subscriptions**:

- **Exclusive Content**: Offer premium content to members, such as in-depth articles, videos, or podcasts. This content should provide significant value to justify the subscription fee.

- **Community Access**: Build a private community where members can interact, share insights, and receive support. Platforms like Patreon or your own site's forum can facilitate this.

- **Perks and Discounts**: Provide members with exclusive perks, such as early access to new products, special discounts, or personalized coaching sessions.

Collaborating with Other Bloggers and Influencers

1. **Guest Blogging**:

- **Expand Your Reach**: Write guest posts for other popular blogs in your niche. This not only introduces your content to a new audience but also builds backlinks to improve your SEO.

- **Invite Guest Bloggers**: Host guest bloggers on your site to provide fresh perspectives and content. This can attract the guest blogger's audience to your site and enhance your content variety.

2. **Influencer Partnerships**:

- **Joint Ventures**: Partner with influencers for joint projects, such as co-authored content, collaborative courses, or joint webinars. These collaborations can leverage each partner's audience for mutual benefit.

- **Social Media Campaigns**: Work with influencers to promote your products or content on social media. Influencers can create authentic content that resonates with their followers and drives traffic to your blog.

3. **Cross-Promotions**:

- **Content Sharing**: Share each other's content on social media, newsletters, or blogs to reach a wider audience. This mutual promotion helps both parties grow their audiences and increase engagement.

- **Affiliate Partnerships**: Partner with other bloggers to promote each other's products through affiliate marketing. This can provide a new revenue stream and strengthen relationships within your niche.

Continuously Optimizing and Updating Content

1. **Content Audit**:

- **Regular Review**: Conduct regular content audits to evaluate the performance of your existing posts. Identify high-performing content and areas that need improvement.

- **Update Information**: Ensure your content remains accurate and relevant by updating outdated information, statistics, and references. This keeps your blog valuable and trustworthy.

2. **SEO Optimization**:

- **Keyword Refresh**: Reevaluate your keywords and update them based on current trends and search behaviors. Use tools like Ahrefs and SEMrush to find new keyword opportunities.

- **Internal Linking**: Improve your internal linking structure to enhance navigation and SEO. Link to related posts within your blog to keep readers engaged and distribute page authority.

3. **Enhancing User Experience**:

- **Improve Readability**: Break up long paragraphs, use bullet points, and add subheadings to make your content more readable. A better user experience increases the time readers spend on your site.

- **Multimedia Integration**: Add images, videos, infographics, and other multimedia elements to make your content more engaging. This can enhance comprehension and retention.

4. **Performance Tracking**:

- **Analytics Tools**: Use tools like Google Analytics and Google Search Console to monitor your blog's performance. Track metrics such as traffic, bounce rate, and conversion rates to gauge the effectiveness of your strategies.

- **A/B Testing**: Conduct A/B tests on different elements of your blog, such as headlines, CTAs, and layout. Use the results to optimize for better performance and higher engagement.

Example Table: Diversifying Blogging Income

Income Stream	Description	Benefits
eBooks	In-depth written content sold as digital downloads	Passive income, authority building
Online Courses	Structured educational content	High revenue potential, engagement
Membership Sites	Recurring subscriptions for exclusive content	Steady income, community building
Guest Blogging	Writing for other blogs to reach new audiences	SEO benefits, brand exposure
Influencer Partnerships	Joint projects and social media campaigns	Audience growth, increased traffic
Content Updates	Regularly refreshing existing posts	Improved SEO, maintained relevance

By diversifying your income streams, collaborating with others in your niche, and continuously optimizing your content, you can effectively scale your blogging income. These strategies not only enhance your revenue potential but also ensure long-term growth and sustainability for your blog. Implementing these approaches will help you build a robust and profitable blogging business.

Chapter 7: Creating and Selling Online Courses

7.1 The Online Course Market

Creating and selling online courses is a powerful way to generate passive income. This section provides an overview of the online education market, explores the benefits of creating and selling online courses, and offers guidance on identifying profitable course topics.

Overview of the Online Education Market

1. **Market Growth**:

- **Expanding Reach**: The online education market has seen tremendous growth over the past decade. According to a report by Global Market Insights, the e-learning market size surpassed USD 200 billion in 2019 and is expected to grow at a compound annual growth rate (CAGR) of over 8% from 2020 to 2026.

- **Accessibility**: Online education offers unparalleled accessibility, allowing learners from all over the world to access high-quality educational content. This has led to a surge in demand for online courses across various fields and industries.

2. **Technological Advancements**:

- **Improved Platforms**: Advances in technology have led to the development of robust online learning platforms such as Udemy, Coursera, and Teachable. These platforms provide tools for course creation, marketing, and delivery, making it easier for educators to reach a global audience.

- **Interactive Learning**: Modern e-learning platforms support interactive elements such as quizzes, discussion forums, and live sessions, enhancing the learning experience and engagement.

3. **Market Segmentation**:

- **Professional Development**: A significant portion of the online education market is dedicated to professional development courses, which help individuals acquire new skills, advance in their careers, and stay competitive in the job market.

- **Academic Courses**: Many online platforms offer academic courses and degrees, partnering with universities to provide accredited programs.

- **Personal Enrichment**: There is also a growing market for courses focused on hobbies, wellness, and personal growth, catering to individuals seeking to improve their personal lives and pursue their passions.

Benefits of Creating and Selling Online Courses

1. **Scalability**:

- **Unlimited Enrollment**: Unlike traditional classroom settings, online courses can accommodate an unlimited number of students. This scalability allows course creators to reach a vast audience without additional costs.

- **Automation**: Once created, online courses can be delivered automatically, reducing the need for ongoing involvement. This allows course creators to generate passive income while focusing on other ventures.

2. **Revenue Potential**:

- **Multiple Income Streams**: Online courses can be sold on various platforms, including your own website, increasing the potential for multiple revenue streams. Additionally, courses can be bundled, offered as part of a membership site, or included in subscription services.

- **High Profit Margins**: With low overhead costs and the ability to reuse and update content, online courses often have high profit margins. After the initial investment in course creation, the ongoing costs are minimal.

3. **Flexibility**:

- **Content Updates**: Online courses can be easily updated to reflect new information and trends, ensuring that the content remains relevant and valuable to learners.

- **Creative Freedom**: Course creators have the flexibility to design and structure their courses in a way that best suits their teaching style and meets the needs of their target audience.

4. **Impact and Reach**:

- **Global Audience**: Online courses can reach learners worldwide, breaking down geographical barriers and expanding the impact of your expertise.

- **Personal Satisfaction**: Sharing knowledge and helping others achieve their goals can be highly rewarding, providing a sense of fulfillment and purpose.

Identifying Profitable Course Topics

1. **Market Research**:

   - **Keyword Research**: Use tools like Google Keyword Planner, Ahrefs, and SEMrush to identify popular search terms related to your expertise. High search volume indicates strong demand for those topics.

   - **Competitor Analysis**: Analyze existing courses in your niche on platforms like Udemy, Coursera, and Teachable. Identify gaps in the market that you can fill with unique or more in-depth content.

2. **Audience Needs**:

   - **Surveys and Feedback**: Engage with your audience through surveys, social media, and email newsletters to understand their needs and interests. Ask them what topics they would like to learn more about and what challenges they face.

   - **Online Communities**: Participate in online forums, groups, and communities related to your niche. Observe common questions and discussions to identify potential course topics.

3. **Your Expertise and Passion**:

   - **Skills Inventory**: Assess your skills, knowledge, and experience to identify areas where you can offer valuable insights and guidance. Choose topics that you are passionate about, as this enthusiasm will translate into better content and engagement.

   - **Unique Angle**: Consider how you can present your course content uniquely. Your perspective, teaching style, and approach can differentiate your course from others in the market.

4. **Validation**:

- **Pilot Courses**: Test your course ideas with pilot courses or workshops. Offer them to a small group at a discounted rate to gather feedback and validate demand before fully developing the course.

- **Pre-Sales**: Launch pre-sales or crowdfunding campaigns to gauge interest and secure funding for course development. This approach also helps build anticipation and a sense of exclusivity.

Example Table: Profitable Course Topics and Platforms

Course Topic	Platform	Target Audience	Revenue Potential
Digital Marketing	Udemy	Entrepreneurs, Marketers	High
Data Science	Coursera	Professionals, Students	High
Personal Finance	Teachable	General Public	Moderate to High
Photography	Skillshare	Hobbyists, Creatives	Moderate
Coding and Programming	Codecademy	Students, Tech Enthusiasts	High

The online course market offers vast opportunities for generating passive income through the creation and sale of educational content. By understanding the market dynamics, leveraging the benefits of online courses, and identifying profitable topics, you can establish a successful and scalable online education business. This strategic approach will not only enhance your income potential but also allow you to make a meaningful impact on a global audience.

7.2 Developing Your Course Content

Creating a successful online course involves meticulously planning your curriculum, producing engaging video and written content, and incorporating quizzes and assignments to enhance the learning experience. This section provides detailed guidance on structuring your course curriculum, creating compelling content, and using interactive elements to improve learner engagement and retention.

Structuring Your Course Curriculum

1. **Defining Learning Objectives**:

   - **Clear Goals**: Start by defining clear learning objectives for your course. Identify what you want your students to achieve by the end of the course. These objectives will guide the content creation process and ensure that each module aligns with the overall goals.

   - **Outcome-Focused**: Frame your objectives in terms of specific outcomes. For example, "Students will be able to create a basic website using HTML and CSS" is more actionable than "Understanding HTML and CSS."

2. **Course Outline**:

   - **Module Breakdown**: Divide your course into modules, each covering a major topic or skill. Ensure each module builds on the previous one to create a logical progression.

   - **Lesson Plans**: Break down each module into individual lessons. Outline the key points, activities, and resources for each lesson. This detailed planning helps maintain focus and ensures comprehensive coverage of each topic.

3. **Balanced Content Delivery**:

- **Variety in Content**: Incorporate a mix of content types to cater to different learning styles. Use videos, written materials, infographics, and interactive elements to keep the course engaging.

- **Pacing and Length**: Consider the pacing and length of each lesson. Aim for lessons that are concise but thorough, typically between 10 to 20 minutes. This helps maintain students' attention and makes the content more digestible.

Creating Engaging Video and Written Content

1. **Video Content**:

- **Script Writing**: Write detailed scripts for your videos to ensure clarity and coherence. A well-structured script helps you stay on track and cover all necessary points.

- **Production Quality**: Invest in good-quality video and audio equipment. Clear visuals and sound significantly enhance the learning experience. Use proper lighting and a clean background to create a professional look.

- **Engagement Techniques**: Use storytelling, real-world examples, and analogies to make the content relatable and interesting. Break up longer videos with visuals, animations, and transitions to keep viewers engaged.

2. **Written Content**:

- **Comprehensive Guides**: Provide detailed written guides to complement your video content. These guides can serve as reference materials that students can revisit.

- **Visual Aids**: Enhance your written content with images, charts, and infographics. Visual aids help explain complex concepts and make the material more engaging.

- **Clarity and Precision**: Use clear and concise language. Avoid jargon unless it is necessary for the topic, and always provide explanations for technical terms.

3. **Interactive Elements**:

- **Discussion Forums**: Set up discussion forums where students can ask questions, share insights, and interact with each other. This fosters a sense of community and collaborative learning.

- **Live Sessions**: Schedule live Q&A sessions or webinars to address students' questions in real-time and provide additional support.

Using Quizzes and Assignments to Enhance Learning

1. **Quizzes**:

- **Knowledge Checks**: Incorporate quizzes at the end of each module to assess understanding and reinforce key concepts. Use a mix of question types, including multiple-choice, true/false, and short answer questions.

- **Immediate Feedback**: Provide immediate feedback on quiz results. Explain the correct answers and why they are correct. This helps students learn from their mistakes and understand the material better.

- **Progress Tracking**: Use quizzes to track students' progress. Identify areas where they may be struggling and offer additional resources or support as needed.

2. **Assignments**:

- **Practical Application**: Design assignments that require students to apply what they have learned. For example, in a web development course, an assignment could involve creating a simple website.

- **Clear Instructions**: Provide clear and detailed instructions for each assignment. Outline the objectives, expected outcomes, and evaluation criteria.

- **Peer Review**: Incorporate peer review as part of the assignment process. This not only allows students to learn from each other but also encourages critical thinking and constructive feedback.

3. **Project-Based Learning**:

- **Capstone Projects**: Include a capstone project that brings together all the skills and knowledge acquired throughout the course. This project should be comprehensive and challenging, allowing students to demonstrate their mastery of the subject.

- **Real-World Relevance**: Design projects that have real-world relevance. This makes the learning experience more meaningful and prepares students for practical application in their careers or personal endeavors.

Example Table: Course Content Development Checklist

Content Type	Key Elements	Best Practices
Video Content	Script, Production Quality, Engagement Techniques	Use high-quality equipment, clear visuals, and sound

Content Type	Key Elements	Best Practices
Written Content	Comprehensive Guides, Visual Aids, Clarity	Include images and infographics, use concise language
Quizzes	Knowledge Checks, Immediate Feedback, Progress Tracking	Mix question types, provide feedback, track progress
Assignments	Practical Application, Clear Instructions, Peer Review	Provide detailed instructions, encourage peer feedback
Projects	Capstone Projects, Real-World Relevance	Ensure comprehensive and challenging, relevant to real-world

Developing effective course content requires careful planning, high-quality production, and interactive elements to ensure an engaging and comprehensive learning experience. By structuring your curriculum thoughtfully, creating compelling video and written content, and incorporating quizzes and assignments, you can create a course that not only educates but also inspires and retains students. This approach will help you establish a reputable and successful online course that generates passive income and delivers value to learners worldwide.

7.3 Choosing the Right Platform

Choosing the right platform is a crucial step in creating and selling online courses. The platform you select will influence the reach, functionality, and user experience of your course. This section explores the evaluation of popular online course platforms, the steps to set up your course, and effective pricing strategies to maximize revenue and attract students.

Evaluating Online Course Platforms

1. **Teachable**:

    - **Features**: Teachable offers robust features for course creation, including customizable templates, multimedia support, and integrated quizzes. It also provides tools for marketing and sales, such as affiliate marketing and email marketing integrations.

    - **User Experience**: Known for its user-friendly interface, Teachable makes it easy for instructors to build and manage courses. Students also benefit from a smooth learning experience with a clean, intuitive design.

    - **Pricing**: Teachable has various pricing plans, starting from a free basic plan with transaction fees to professional plans with more features and lower fees.

2. **Udemy**:

    - **Marketplace Reach**: Udemy is a massive online learning marketplace with millions of students. It offers a wide range of courses and has a large built-in audience, making it easier to attract students without extensive marketing.

    - **Course Creation Tools**: Udemy provides comprehensive tools for creating courses, including video hosting, quizzes, and certificates of completion. It also offers marketing support through promotions and targeted emails.

- **Revenue Sharing**: Udemy operates on a revenue-sharing model, where instructors receive a percentage of the course sales. This can be beneficial for those who prefer to leverage Udemy's marketing efforts but might result in lower margins compared to other platforms.

3. **Thinkific**:

- **Customization and Control**: Thinkific offers extensive customization options, allowing you to create a branded learning environment. You can design your course site, control pricing, and manage student data.

- **Support and Resources**: Thinkific provides robust support and resources for course creators, including webinars, tutorials, and a dedicated support team.

- **Pricing**: Thinkific offers a free plan with limited features and several paid plans that provide more advanced options and increased support.

4. **Kajabi**:

- **All-in-One Solution**: Kajabi is an all-in-one platform that combines course creation, marketing, and sales tools. It offers features like website building, email marketing, and automation.

- **Professional Appearance**: Kajabi is known for its high-quality design and professional appearance, making it ideal for course creators looking to establish a premium brand.

- **Pricing**: Kajabi is more expensive than other platforms, with plans starting at a higher price point. However, its comprehensive feature set can justify the cost for those looking to manage all aspects of their online business from a single platform.

Setting Up Your Course on the Chosen Platform

1. **Course Structure and Content Upload**:

- **Curriculum Layout**: Organize your course content into modules and lessons. Ensure a logical flow that guides students through the material progressively.

- **Multimedia Integration**: Upload videos, PDFs, quizzes, and other multimedia content. Use the platform's tools to ensure each piece of content is formatted correctly and accessible.

2. **Customization and Branding**:

- **Custom Themes**: Select and customize themes that align with your brand. Adjust colors, fonts, and layouts to create a cohesive and professional look.

- **Branding Elements**: Add your logo, brand colors, and other visual elements to reinforce your brand identity throughout the course.

3. **Engagement and Interaction**:

- **Discussion Forums**: Set up discussion forums or comment sections for students to interact, ask questions, and engage with the material.

- **Live Sessions**: Integrate live webinars or Q&A sessions to provide real-time interaction and support.

4. **Marketing and Sales Tools**:

- **Landing Pages**: Create compelling landing pages to promote your course. Highlight key benefits, include testimonials, and use clear calls-to-action.

- **Email Marketing**: Set up email campaigns to nurture leads and convert them into students. Use automated sequences to welcome new students and keep them engaged.

Pricing Strategies for Online Courses

1. **Market Research and Competitor Analysis**:

- **Competitive Pricing**: Analyze the pricing of similar courses on your chosen platform and other platforms. Position your course competitively while considering the value you provide.

- **Value Proposition**: Highlight the unique aspects of your course that justify your pricing. This could include exclusive content, expert instruction, or additional resources.

2. **Tiered Pricing**:

- **Multiple Tiers**: Offer different pricing tiers with varying levels of access and features. For example, a basic tier might include the core course content, while a premium tier includes additional resources, live sessions, and personalized feedback.

- **Bundling Options**: Bundle your course with other products or services, such as eBooks, one-on-one coaching, or membership access. This adds value and incentivizes higher-tier purchases.

3. **Promotional Pricing**:

- **Early Bird Discounts**: Offer early bird pricing for students who enroll before the official launch. This creates urgency and encourages early sign-ups.

- **Seasonal Promotions**: Run promotions during holidays, back-to-school periods, or other significant times to boost enrollment. Use limited-time offers to create a sense of urgency.

4. **Payment Plans**:

- **Installment Payments**: Offer payment plans that allow students to pay in installments rather than a lump sum. This makes your course more accessible to a wider audience and can increase overall sales.

- **Subscription Models**: Consider a subscription model where students pay a recurring fee for ongoing access to your course and additional content.

Example Table: Platform Comparison

Platform	Key Features	Pricing	Best For
Teachable	Customizable templates, marketing tools, quizzes	Free basic plan, paid plans start at $29/month	Beginners, diverse courses
Udemy	Large marketplace, extensive reach, marketing support	Revenue sharing model	Wide audience, leveraging platform's marketing

Platform	Key Features	Pricing	Best For
Thinkific	Customization, support resources, control over pricing	Free plan, paid plans start at $39/month	Full control, advanced customization
Kajabi	All-in-one solution, high-quality design, automation	Paid plans start at $119/month	Professional, premium brands

Choosing the right platform for your online course involves evaluating the features, pricing, and target audience of each option. By setting up your course effectively and implementing strategic pricing, you can maximize your reach and revenue potential. This approach will help you establish a successful and sustainable online course business, providing value to learners while generating passive income.

7.4 Marketing and Selling Your Course

Successfully marketing and selling your online course is essential for reaching your target audience and converting leads into paying students. This section outlines effective strategies for promoting your course, converting leads, and leveraging testimonials and reviews to build credibility.

Strategies for Promoting Your Course

1. **Email Marketing**:

   - **Building Your List**: Start by building an email list of potential students. Offer a free resource or lead magnet, such as a mini-course, eBook, or checklist, in exchange for email sign-ups.

- **Nurture Campaigns**: Create a series of automated emails to nurture your leads. Provide valuable content, insights, and tips related to your course topic to build trust and demonstrate your expertise.

- **Launch Emails**: When you're ready to launch, send a series of promotional emails to your list. Highlight the benefits of your course, include testimonials, and offer limited-time discounts to encourage sign-ups.

2. **Social Media Marketing**:

- **Platform Selection**: Choose social media platforms where your target audience is most active. Focus on 2-3 platforms to start, such as Facebook, Instagram, LinkedIn, or Twitter.

- **Content Strategy**: Develop a content strategy that includes regular posts, stories, and videos about your course. Share behind-the-scenes looks, student success stories, and snippets of your course content.

- **Advertising**: Use paid social media ads to reach a broader audience. Platforms like Facebook and Instagram offer advanced targeting options, allowing you to reach potential students based on their interests, behaviors, and demographics.

3. **Webinars and Live Sessions**:

- **Hosting Webinars**: Host free webinars or live sessions to showcase your expertise and provide a taste of what students can expect from your course. This helps build trust and rapport with your audience.

- **Interactive Engagement**: Encourage interaction during your webinars by answering questions, conducting polls, and offering live feedback. This keeps your audience engaged and increases their interest in your course.

- **Follow-Up**: After the webinar, follow up with attendees via email. Provide a special offer or discount for your course to incentivize them to enroll.

4. **Content Marketing**:

- **Blogging**: Write blog posts related to your course topic. Optimize your posts for SEO to attract organic traffic from search engines. Include calls to action (CTAs) that direct readers to your course landing page.

- **Guest Blogging**: Write guest posts for other blogs in your niche. This exposes your content to a new audience and helps build backlinks to your site, improving your SEO.

- **Video Content**: Create informative and engaging videos for platforms like YouTube. Use these videos to provide value, showcase your teaching style, and direct viewers to your course.

Converting Leads into Paying Students

1. **Clear and Compelling Landing Pages**:

- **Course Benefits**: Highlight the key benefits and outcomes of your course on your landing page. Use bullet points, clear headlines, and compelling visuals to convey the value.

- **Course Details**: Provide detailed information about your course content, structure, and what students will learn. Include a curriculum outline and any prerequisites.

- **Call to Action**: Use strong CTAs that encourage visitors to enroll. Phrases like "Join Now," "Get Started," or "Enroll Today" create a sense of urgency.

2. **Limited-Time Offers and Discounts**:

- **Early Bird Discounts**: Offer early bird pricing for a limited time to encourage quick sign-ups. This creates urgency and rewards those who commit early.

- **Bundle Deals**: Bundle your course with other products or services, such as eBooks, one-on-one coaching sessions, or additional courses. This adds value and makes the purchase more attractive.

- **Seasonal Promotions**: Run seasonal promotions during holidays, back-to-school periods, or other significant times. Use these promotions to boost enrollment and create a sense of urgency.

3. **Personalized Follow-Ups**:

- **Email Follow-Ups**: Follow up with leads who have shown interest but haven't enrolled. Send personalized emails addressing their specific needs and concerns, and offer incentives to encourage them to sign up.

- **Retargeting Ads**: Use retargeting ads to reach people who have visited your course landing page but didn't enroll. These ads serve as reminders and can include special offers to entice them back.

Using Testimonials and Reviews to Build Credibility

1. **Collecting Testimonials**:

- **Student Feedback**: Reach out to your students for feedback and testimonials. Ask them to share their experiences and the benefits they've gained from your course.

- **Video Testimonials**: Encourage students to provide video testimonials. Videos are more personal and can be more persuasive than written reviews.

2. **Showcasing Testimonials**:

- **Landing Pages**: Display testimonials prominently on your course landing page. Include photos of the students (with their permission) to add authenticity.

- **Social Proof**: Share testimonials on your social media channels, in your email marketing, and within your course promotion materials. Highlight specific success stories and transformative experiences.

3. **Encouraging Reviews**:

- **Review Requests**: Ask your students to leave reviews on your course platform or website. Make it easy for them by providing direct links and simple instructions.

- **Incentives**: Offer incentives for leaving reviews, such as discounts on future courses or access to exclusive content. This encourages more students to share their positive experiences.

Example Table: Marketing Strategies and Tools

Strategy	Tools/Platforms	Key Actions
Email Marketing	Mailchimp, ConvertKit, AWeber	Build list, nurture campaigns, launch emails
Social Media Marketing	Facebook, Instagram, LinkedIn, Twitter	Regular posts, stories, paid ads

Strategy	Tools/Platforms	Key Actions
Webinars and Live Sessions	Zoom, GoToWebinar, Facebook Live	Host webinars, engage interactively, follow-up emails
Content Marketing	WordPress, Medium, YouTube	Blogging, guest posts, video content
Retargeting Ads	Google Ads, Facebook Ads	Target past visitors, offer special deals
Testimonials and Reviews	Your course platform, Social Media	Collect feedback, display prominently, incentivize reviews

Effectively marketing and selling your course involves a combination of strategies to reach and convert potential students. By leveraging email marketing, social media, webinars, and content marketing, you can attract a broad audience. Converting these leads into paying students requires clear communication of your course's value, personalized follow-ups, and strategic offers. Finally, using testimonials and reviews builds credibility and trust, encouraging more enrollments and long-term success for your online course.

7.5 Scaling Your Online Course Business

Scaling your online course business involves expanding your offerings, increasing your reach, and continuously improving your content. This section outlines strategies for creating a portfolio of courses, expanding through partnerships, and regularly updating and enhancing your course material to ensure ongoing growth and success.

Creating a Portfolio of Courses

1. **Diversifying Course Topics**:

- **Complementary Subjects**: Develop courses on subjects that complement your initial course. For example, if your first course is about basic digital marketing, you could create additional courses on advanced SEO, social media marketing, and email marketing.

- **Audience Demand**: Listen to your audience's needs and requests. Conduct surveys and analyze feedback to identify new topics that your existing students are interested in.

2. **Course Series and Bundles**:

- **Sequential Learning**: Create a series of courses that take students from beginner to advanced levels. This encourages students to continue their education with you, increasing lifetime customer value.

- **Course Bundles**: Offer course bundles at a discounted rate. Bundling courses together can provide a comprehensive learning experience and incentivize students to purchase more.

3. **Certification Programs**:

- **Accreditation**: Develop certification programs for your courses. Offering a certification upon completion can make your courses more appealing, especially to professionals looking to enhance their credentials.

- **Continuing Education**: Partner with professional organizations to offer continuing education credits for your courses. This can attract professionals who need to maintain their certifications.

Expanding Your Reach Through Partnerships

1. **Strategic Alliances**:

- **Industry Experts**: Collaborate with industry experts and influencers to co-create courses. Their expertise and following can lend credibility to your courses and attract a wider audience.

- **Educational Institutions**: Partner with universities and colleges to offer your courses as part of their continuing education programs. This can significantly expand your reach and credibility.

2. **Affiliate Programs**:

- **Affiliate Marketing**: Establish an affiliate program to incentivize others to promote your courses. Affiliates earn a commission for each sale they refer, expanding your marketing efforts without upfront costs.

- **Collaborative Promotions**: Work with affiliates to create joint marketing campaigns. For example, you could co-host a webinar with an affiliate, providing valuable content and promoting your course to their audience.

3. **Corporate Training**:

- **Business Partnerships**: Offer your courses as corporate training solutions. Tailor your courses to meet the specific needs of businesses and offer bulk enrollment discounts.

- **Employee Development**: Market your courses as part of employee development programs. Companies invest in training to enhance their workforce's skills, providing a steady stream of students for your courses.

Continuously Updating and Improving Course Content

1. **Regular Content Reviews**:

- **Feedback Analysis**: Collect and analyze feedback from students to identify areas for improvement. Regularly update your courses based on this feedback to ensure they remain relevant and valuable.

- **Industry Trends**: Stay up-to-date with the latest industry trends and advancements. Incorporate new developments into your courses to keep the content current and competitive.

2. **Enhanced Learning Materials**:

- **Multimedia Integration**: Continuously enhance your courses with new multimedia elements, such as updated videos, interactive simulations, and infographics. These elements can make your courses more engaging and effective.

- **Supplementary Resources**: Provide additional resources, such as downloadable templates, guides, and reading materials. These resources can enhance the learning experience and provide extra value to students.

3. **Advanced Features and Interactivity**:

- **Interactive Quizzes and Assignments**: Add new quizzes and assignments to assess student progress and reinforce learning. Interactive elements keep students engaged and help them retain information.

- **Live Sessions and Q&A**: Incorporate regular live sessions and Q&A with instructors. This allows students to clarify doubts and interact with the course creators, enhancing their learning experience.

4. **Technology and Platform Upgrades**:

- **Platform Enhancements**: Regularly upgrade your course platform to take advantage of new features and improve user experience. Ensure the platform is mobile-friendly and accessible to all students.

- **AI and Analytics**: Utilize AI and analytics tools to track student progress and performance. Use these insights to personalize the learning experience and identify areas for improvement.

Example Table: Strategies for Scaling Your Online Course Business

Strategy	Actions	Benefits
Diversifying Course Topics	Develop complementary courses, survey audience for new topics	Increased revenue, broader audience
Course Series and Bundles	Create sequential courses, offer bundles at a discount	Higher customer lifetime value
Certification Programs	Develop accredited certification programs	Enhanced course appeal, professional credibility
Strategic Alliances	Partner with industry experts, educational institutions	Expanded reach, increased credibility

Strategy	Actions	Benefits
Affiliate Programs	Establish affiliate marketing, collaborative promotions	Cost-effective marketing, wider reach
Corporate Training	Offer courses to businesses, tailor to corporate needs	Steady student stream, bulk enrollments
Regular Content Reviews	Analyze feedback, update content based on industry trends	Relevance, continuous improvement
Enhanced Learning Materials	Integrate multimedia, provide supplementary resources	Engaging content, added value
Advanced Features and Interactivity	Add quizzes, assignments, live sessions	Improved learning experience, engagement
Technology and Platform Upgrades	Upgrade platform features, utilize AI and analytics tools	Better user experience, personalized learning

Scaling your online course business requires a strategic approach to diversifying your course offerings, leveraging partnerships, and continuously enhancing your content. By creating a portfolio of courses, expanding your reach through collaborations, and maintaining high-quality, updated content, you can ensure sustainable growth and success in the competitive online education market. This comprehensive strategy will help you attract more students, increase your revenue, and establish your brand as a leader in your niche.

Chapter 8: Writing and Self-Publishing E-books

8.1 Introduction to Self-Publishing

Self-publishing has revolutionized the publishing industry, making it accessible for authors to publish their work independently. This section explores the self-publishing industry, highlights the benefits of self-publishing e-books, and provides guidance on choosing a profitable book topic.

Overview of the Self-Publishing Industry

1. **Industry Growth**:

   - **Rapid Expansion**: The self-publishing industry has experienced significant growth over the past decade. Advances in technology and the rise of digital platforms like Amazon Kindle Direct Publishing (KDP) have made it easier than ever for authors to publish and distribute their work.

   - **Market Size**: According to Bowker, the number of self-published titles in the U.S. has grown dramatically, with millions of new titles released each year. This growth indicates a robust market with substantial opportunities for aspiring authors.

2. **Accessibility and Democratization**:

   - **No Gatekeepers**: Traditional publishing often involves rigorous gatekeeping, with publishers and agents deciding which books get published. Self-publishing bypasses these gatekeepers, allowing anyone with a story or knowledge to share it with the world.

   - **Ease of Entry**: Platforms like Amazon KDP, IngramSpark, and Smashwords provide user-friendly tools for formatting, publishing, and distributing e-books and print-on-demand books. This ease of entry has lowered barriers for new authors.

3. **Diverse Genres and Niches**:

- **Variety of Genres**: Self-publishing supports a wide range of genres and niches, from fiction and non-fiction to poetry, memoirs, and specialized instructional guides. Authors can find and cater to specific audiences more effectively.

- **Global Reach**: Self-published books are available to a global audience, expanding the potential market beyond traditional local or national boundaries.

Benefits of Self-Publishing E-Books

1. **Creative Control**:

- **Complete Autonomy**: Authors have complete control over every aspect of their book, from writing and editing to cover design and marketing. This autonomy allows for a more personalized and authentic representation of the author's vision.

- **Flexibility**: Self-publishing enables authors to make changes or updates to their work at any time, ensuring the content remains relevant and accurate.

2. **Higher Royalties**:

- **Better Earnings**: Self-published authors typically earn higher royalties compared to those who publish traditionally. For example, Amazon KDP offers up to 70% royalties on e-book sales, whereas traditional publishing contracts often offer around 10-15%.

- **Direct Sales**: Authors can sell their books directly through their own websites or platforms, keeping a larger share of the profits and building a direct relationship with their readers.

3. **Faster Time to Market**:

- **Quick Publication**: Traditional publishing can take years from manuscript submission to book release. Self-publishing significantly shortens this timeline, allowing authors to publish their work as soon as it is ready.

- **Timely Content**: This speed is particularly advantageous for non-fiction works that address current trends or events, ensuring the content is timely and relevant.

4. **Marketing and Branding Opportunities**:

- **Personal Branding**: Self-publishing provides an opportunity for authors to build their personal brand. Authors can create websites, blogs, and social media profiles to engage with their audience and promote their books.

- **Creative Marketing**: Authors can experiment with various marketing strategies, such as email newsletters, book trailers, and collaborations with influencers, to find what works best for their audience.

Choosing a Profitable Book Topic

1. **Market Research**:

- **Identify Trends**: Use tools like Google Trends, Amazon Best Sellers, and Goodreads to identify popular topics and genres. Look for emerging trends and areas with high demand but limited supply.

- **Competitor Analysis**: Analyze successful self-published books in your niche. Examine their titles, cover designs, and reviews to understand what resonates with readers. Identify gaps that your book could fill.

2. **Audience Identification**:

- **Target Demographic**: Define your target audience based on factors such as age, gender, interests, and reading habits.

Understanding your audience helps tailor your content to meet their needs and preferences.

- **Reader Engagement**: Engage with potential readers through social media, forums, and surveys to gather insights into their preferences and pain points. Use this feedback to shape your book's content and marketing strategy.

3. **Personal Passion and Expertise**:

- **Write What You Know**: Choose a topic you are passionate about and knowledgeable in. Writing from personal experience or expertise not only makes the process more enjoyable but also adds credibility to your work.

- **Unique Perspective**: Offer a unique perspective or angle on a popular topic. Differentiating your book from others in the market can attract readers looking for fresh insights.

4. **Feasibility and Scope**:

- **Scope of Content**: Ensure your topic has enough depth to sustain a full-length book. Outline your ideas to check if you have sufficient content to cover the topic comprehensively.

- **Feasibility Study**: Conduct a feasibility study to assess the viability of your book idea. Consider factors such as potential readership, competition, and profitability.

Example Table: Factors to Consider When Choosing a Book Topic

Factor	Description	Tools/Methods
Market Trends	Popular and emerging topics in the market	Google Trends, Amazon Best Sellers, Goodreads

Factor	Description	Tools/Methods
Competition	Analysis of successful books in the same niche	Competitor research, review analysis
Target Audience	Demographic and psychographic profile of potential readers	Social media insights, surveys, forums
Author's Expertise	Personal knowledge and passion for the topic	Self-assessment, expertise mapping
Content Scope	Depth and breadth of the topic for a full-length book	Outlining, brainstorming sessions

Self-publishing offers a unique and accessible opportunity for authors to share their work with a global audience while retaining creative control and earning higher royalties. By understanding the dynamics of the self-publishing industry, leveraging its benefits, and choosing a profitable book topic through thorough research and audience engagement, you can successfully navigate the self-publishing landscape and achieve significant financial and personal rewards.

8.2 Writing Your E-book

Writing an e-book involves meticulous planning, effective writing techniques, and thorough editing and proofreading. This section outlines the key steps in planning and outlining your book, provides writing tips and techniques to keep your content engaging, and discusses the importance of editing and proofreading your manuscript.

Planning and Outlining Your Book

1. **Define Your Purpose and Audience**:

   - **Purpose**: Clearly define the purpose of your e-book. Are you providing valuable information, sharing personal experiences, or teaching a new skill? Understanding your purpose will guide the tone and structure of your book.

   - **Audience**: Identify your target audience. Knowing who your readers are will help you tailor your content to their interests and needs. Consider factors such as age, profession, interests, and knowledge level.

2. **Research and Brainstorm**:

   - **Topic Research**: Conduct thorough research on your chosen topic. Gather information from reputable sources to ensure accuracy and depth. Look at similar books in your genre to identify gaps that your book could fill.

   - **Brainstorming**: Brainstorm ideas and jot down everything that comes to mind. Use mind maps or lists to organize your thoughts and identify key themes and subtopics.

3. **Create an Outline**:

   - **Structure**: Develop a clear structure for your e-book. Typically, an e-book consists of an introduction, several chapters or sections, and a conclusion. Each chapter should cover a specific aspect of your topic.

   - **Chapter Summaries**: Write brief summaries for each chapter. These summaries will serve as a guide when you start writing, ensuring that each chapter stays focused on its main points.

   - **Detailed Outline**: Expand your chapter summaries into a detailed outline. Include key points, subtopics, and examples you want to cover in each chapter. A detailed outline helps maintain a logical flow and makes the writing process more manageable.

Writing Tips and Techniques

1. **Set a Writing Schedule**:

- **Consistency**: Establish a regular writing schedule to maintain momentum. Whether it's daily or weekly, consistency is key to making steady progress.

- **Goals**: Set specific writing goals, such as word count targets for each session. This keeps you focused and motivated.

2. **Write Engaging Content**:

- **Clear and Concise**: Write in a clear and concise manner. Avoid unnecessary jargon and complex sentences. Aim for simplicity and clarity to make your content accessible to a wider audience.

- **Active Voice**: Use active voice instead of passive voice. Active voice makes your writing more direct and engaging. For example, "The author explains" is more engaging than "It is explained by the author."

- **Show, Don't Tell**: Use examples, anecdotes, and case studies to illustrate your points. Showing rather than telling makes your content more relatable and compelling.

3. **Stay Organized**:

- **Sections and Subsections**: Use headings, subheadings, and bullet points to break up your text. This makes your e-book easier to navigate and helps readers quickly find the information they need.

- **Transitions**: Ensure smooth transitions between sections and chapters. Use transitional phrases to maintain the flow and coherence of your writing.

4. **Revise and Refine**:

- **First Draft**: Focus on getting your ideas down in the first draft without worrying too much about perfection. The goal is to get your thoughts on paper.

- **Revisions**: After completing the first draft, revise your content to improve clarity, coherence, and readability. Look for areas where you can add more detail or simplify complex ideas.

Editing and Proofreading Your Manuscript

1. **Self-Editing**:

- **Content Review**: Review your manuscript for content accuracy and completeness. Ensure that all key points are covered and that the information is accurate and up-to-date.

- **Clarity and Flow**: Edit for clarity and logical flow. Remove any redundant or irrelevant content. Ensure that each chapter transitions smoothly to the next.

- **Language and Style**: Check for consistency in language and style. Ensure that your tone remains consistent throughout the book. Adjust the language to suit your target audience.

2. **Professional Editing**:

- **Hiring an Editor**: Consider hiring a professional editor to review your manuscript. A professional editor can provide valuable feedback on structure, content, and language.

- **Types of Editing**: There are different levels of editing, including developmental editing (focuses on structure and content), copy editing (focuses on language and style), and proofreading (focuses on grammar and typos). Depending on your needs, you may require one or more of these services.

3. **Proofreading**:

- **Final Review**: Conduct a final review to catch any remaining errors. Pay attention to grammar, spelling, punctuation, and formatting.

- **Read Aloud**: Reading your manuscript aloud can help you identify awkward sentences and errors that you might miss when reading silently.

- **Beta Readers**: Consider sharing your manuscript with beta readers. Beta readers can provide fresh perspectives and identify areas for improvement that you may have overlooked.

Example Table: Steps for Writing and Editing Your E-book

Step	Action	Details
Planning	Define Purpose and Audience	Understand the goal of your book and who it's for
Research	Conduct Topic Research	Gather information from reputable sources
Outlining	Create Detailed Outline	Structure your book with chapter summaries
Writing	Set a Writing Schedule	Establish regular writing times and goals
Engaging Content	Write Clear and Concise Content	Use active voice and illustrative examples
Organization	Use Sections and Subsections	Break up text for readability
Revisions	Revise for Clarity and Coherence	Improve logical flow and detail

Step	Action	Details
Self-Editing	Review Content and Language	Ensure accuracy and consistency
Professional Editing	Hire an Editor	Get feedback on structure, content, and style
Proofreading	Conduct Final Review	Check for grammar, spelling, and formatting errors

Writing an e-book requires careful planning, disciplined writing, and thorough editing. By following these steps, you can create a well-structured, engaging, and professionally polished e-book that meets the needs of your target audience and stands out in the competitive market.

8.3 Designing and Formatting Your E-book

Designing and formatting your e-book are crucial steps to ensure it is visually appealing and user-friendly. This section covers how to create a professional book cover, format your e-book for various platforms, and use tools and software for book design.

Creating a Professional Book Cover

1. **Importance of a Good Cover**:

- **First Impressions**: Your book cover is the first thing potential readers see. A professional and attractive cover can grab attention and entice readers to explore further.
- **Branding**: A well-designed cover reflects the quality of the content inside and reinforces your brand as an author. It helps establish credibility and professionalism.

2. **Elements of a Professional Cover**:

- **Title and Subtitle**: Ensure your title and subtitle are clear, legible, and prominently displayed. Use a font that is easy to read and stands out against the background.

- **Imagery and Graphics**: Choose images or graphics that are relevant to your book's content. Avoid clutter and focus on a clean, impactful design that conveys the theme of your book.

- **Color Scheme**: Use a color scheme that complements your genre and appeals to your target audience. Colors evoke emotions and can influence a reader's perception of your book.

- **Author Name**: Include your name on the cover, especially if you have established a brand or have multiple books. Make sure it is readable but doesn't overshadow the title.

3. **Design Options**:

- **DIY Design**: If you have design skills, you can create your cover using software like Adobe Photoshop or Canva. These tools offer templates and design elements that can help you craft a professional-looking cover.

- **Professional Designers**: Hiring a professional designer can be a worthwhile investment. Platforms like 99designs, Fiverr, and Upwork connect you with experienced designers who can create a custom cover tailored to your book.

Formatting Your E-book for Various Platforms

1. **Platform-Specific Requirements**:

- **Amazon Kindle (KDP)**: Amazon Kindle Direct Publishing requires e-books to be in MOBI or EPUB format. Ensure your book meets their formatting guidelines, including table of contents, proper metadata, and correct file size.

- **Apple Books**: Apple Books also accepts EPUB files. Ensure your e-book is properly formatted for Apple's platform, including cover image specifications and embedded fonts.
- **Other Platforms**: Platforms like Barnes & Noble Press, Kobo, and Google Play Books have their own formatting guidelines. Always check each platform's requirements to ensure compatibility.

2. **Formatting Elements**:

- **Table of Contents**: Create a clickable table of contents to make navigation easy for readers. This is especially important for non-fiction books with multiple sections and chapters.
- **Headers and Footers**: Use consistent headers and footers for chapter titles and page numbers. This helps maintain a professional look throughout your e-book.
- **Paragraph Styles**: Ensure consistent paragraph styles, including font size, line spacing, and indentation. Avoid using too many different fonts and styles, which can make your book look unprofessional.
- **Images and Graphics**: Optimize images for digital formats by reducing file size without compromising quality. Use appropriate file formats like JPEG or PNG and ensure images are properly aligned with the text.

3. **Tools for Formatting**:

- **Calibre**: Calibre is a free e-book management tool that allows you to convert and format e-books in various formats, including MOBI and EPUB. It also provides features for editing metadata and creating tables of contents.
- **Scrivener**: Scrivener is a writing and organizing tool that includes robust formatting options for e-books. It allows

you to compile your manuscript into multiple formats, ensuring compatibility with different e-book platforms.

- **Vellum**: Vellum is a premium tool designed specifically for formatting e-books and print books. It offers a user-friendly interface and produces beautifully formatted e-books that meet the requirements of major platforms.

Using Tools and Software for Book Design

1. **Design Software**:

- **Adobe InDesign**: Adobe InDesign is a professional desktop publishing software widely used for designing e-books. It offers advanced layout and design features, making it ideal for complex e-books with extensive formatting needs.

- **Canva**: Canva is an online graphic design tool that is beginner-friendly and offers a range of templates and design elements. It is suitable for creating simple e-book covers and graphics.

2. **E-book Conversion Tools**:

- **Kindle Create**: Kindle Create is an official tool from Amazon that helps you format your e-book for Kindle devices. It offers templates and guides you through the process of formatting your manuscript and adding interactive elements.

- **Reedsy Book Editor**: Reedsy's online book editor allows you to write, format, and export your e-book in various formats. It provides a clean interface and is designed to produce professional-quality e-books.

3. **Cover Design Tools**:

- **BookBrush**: BookBrush is a tool specifically designed for creating book covers and marketing graphics. It offers templates, 3D book mockups, and customization options tailored to authors.

- **Placeit**: Placeit provides mockup and design templates for book covers, promotional materials, and social media graphics. It is user-friendly and requires no design experience.

Example Table: Tools for Designing and Formatting Your E-book

Tool	Purpose	Features	Pricing
Adobe InDesign	Book Design	Advanced layout, typography, and design tools	Subscription-based
Canva	Cover Design, Graphics	Templates, drag-and-drop interface	Free, with paid options
Calibre	E-book Conversion, Formatting	Converts between formats, manages e-book library	Free
Scrivener	Writing, Formatting	Manuscript organization, compile for e-book formats	One-time purchase
Vellum	E-book Formatting	User-friendly interface, professional output	One-time purchase
Kindle Create	Kindle Formatting	Templates, guides for Kindle formatting	Free
Reedsy Book Editor	Writing, Formatting	Online editor, exports in various formats	Free

Tool	Purpose	Features	Pricing
BookBrush	Cover Design, Marketing	Templates, 3D book mockups, customization	Subscription-based
Placeit	Cover and Promo Design	Mockup and design templates	Subscription-based

Designing and formatting your e-book to a professional standard is essential for making a positive impression on readers and ensuring compatibility with various e-book platforms. By creating a compelling book cover, following platform-specific formatting guidelines, and utilizing the right tools and software, you can produce a high-quality e-book that stands out in the competitive market.

8.4 Publishing Your E-book

Publishing your e-book is a critical step in bringing your work to market and making it available to readers worldwide. This section covers choosing the right self-publishing platform, the process of uploading and publishing your e-book, and setting the right price to attract readers and maximize profits.

Choosing the Right Self-Publishing Platform

1. **Amazon Kindle Direct Publishing (KDP)**:

- **Market Leader**: Amazon KDP is the most popular self-publishing platform, offering access to millions of readers worldwide. It provides a range of tools and resources to help authors publish and promote their books.

- **Royalties**: KDP offers competitive royalty rates of 35% or 70%, depending on the price of your e-book and the distribution options you choose. The 70% royalty option is available for e-books priced between $2.99 and $9.99.

- **KDP Select**: Enrolling in KDP Select gives your book exclusive benefits, such as participation in Kindle Unlimited and Kindle Owners' Lending Library, which can increase your book's visibility and earnings.

2. **Smashwords**:

- **Wide Distribution**: Smashwords distributes e-books to multiple retailers, including Apple Books, Barnes & Noble, Kobo, and many others. This wide distribution network helps you reach a broader audience.

- **Formatting Requirements**: Smashwords has specific formatting guidelines, known as the Smashwords Style Guide, which must be followed for your e-book to be accepted. Proper formatting ensures your book is compatible with various retailers.

- **Royalty Rates**: Smashwords offers up to 80% royalties on sales through its platform and around 60% on sales through its distribution network.

3. **IngramSpark**:

- **Print and E-book Distribution**: IngramSpark offers both print-on-demand and e-book distribution services. This makes it a good choice for authors who want to publish both digital and print versions of their books.

- **Global Reach**: IngramSpark provides access to a global distribution network, including online retailers, bookstores, and libraries.

- **Costs**: Unlike KDP, IngramSpark charges a setup fee for publishing your book. However, the extensive distribution options can justify the cost.

4. **Other Platforms**:

- **Barnes & Noble Press**: Ideal for reaching readers who prefer Barnes & Noble. Offers competitive royalty rates and easy publishing tools.

- **Kobo Writing Life**: Targets a global audience with strong market presence in Canada, Europe, and Australia. Offers up to 70% royalties.

Uploading and Publishing Your E-book

1. **Preparing Your Files**:

- **Final Manuscript**: Ensure your manuscript is properly formatted and free of errors. Convert it to the appropriate file format (usually MOBI for Kindle, EPUB for others).

- **Cover Design**: Prepare a high-resolution cover image that meets the platform's specifications. The cover should be attractive and professional.

2. **Metadata and Keywords**:

- **Title and Subtitle**: Choose a clear, descriptive title and subtitle that include relevant keywords to improve discoverability.

- **Author Name**: Ensure your author name is consistent across all platforms to build your brand.

- **Description**: Write a compelling book description that highlights the key benefits and hooks potential readers. Use keywords strategically to enhance searchability.

- **Categories and Keywords**: Select appropriate categories and keywords to help your book appear in relevant searches. Research popular categories in your genre and choose keywords that potential readers are likely to use.

3. **Uploading to the Platform**:

- **Create an Account**: If you haven't already, create an account on your chosen self-publishing platform.

- **Upload Files**: Follow the platform's instructions to upload your manuscript and cover file. Verify that the files meet the required specifications.

- **Set Up Metadata**: Enter your book's metadata, including title, author name, description, categories, and keywords. Ensure all information is accurate and optimized for searchability.

4. **Review and Publish**:

- **Preview**: Use the platform's preview tool to check how your e-book will look on various devices. Make any necessary adjustments to ensure a polished final product.

- **Rights and Pricing**: Set the territories where you hold distribution rights and choose the royalty option. Set your book's price, considering market norms and your revenue goals.

- **Publish**: Once you're satisfied with everything, click the publish button. Your book will go through a review process before becoming available for purchase.

Setting the Right Price for Your Book

1. **Market Research**:

- **Competitor Analysis**: Research similar books in your genre to understand the typical price range. Pricing your book competitively can help attract readers.

- **Reader Expectations**: Consider what your target audience expects to pay for an e-book in your genre. Pricing too high or too low can affect sales and perceived value.

2. **Pricing Strategies**:

- **Introductory Pricing**: Launch your book at a lower price to encourage early sales and build momentum. You can gradually increase the price as your book gains reviews and visibility.

- **Free Promotions**: Offering your book for free for a limited time can increase downloads and reviews. This strategy is particularly effective if you have a series of books.

- **Discounts and Promotions**: Regularly offer discounts or participate in promotional events to boost sales. Use promotional tools provided by platforms like KDP Select to increase visibility.

3. **Value-Based Pricing**:

- **Content Quality**: Ensure your book offers high-quality content that justifies the price. Well-written, well-edited, and professionally designed books can command higher prices.

- **Additional Content**: Consider including bonus content, such as a reader's guide, interview with the author, or additional chapters, to enhance value.

Example Table: Comparison of Self-Publishing Platforms

Platform	Key Features	Royalty Rates	Best For
Amazon KDP	Largest market reach, KDP Select benefits	35% or 70%	Wide audience, Kindle users
Smashwords	Wide distribution network, high royalties	Up to 80% (Smashwords), ~60% (retailers)	Broad reach, multiple retailers

Platform	Key Features	Royalty Rates	Best For
IngramSpark	Print and e-book distribution, global reach	Varies by retailer	Print and digital, global distribution
Barnes & Noble Press	Easy publishing, competitive royalties	Up to 65%	B&N readers, U.S. market
Kobo Writing Life	Strong international presence, promotional tools	Up to 70%	Global reach, non-Amazon markets

Publishing your e-book involves selecting the right platform, preparing and uploading your files, and setting a competitive price. By carefully considering each of these steps, you can maximize your e-book's visibility and sales, ensuring a successful launch and sustained success in the self-publishing market.

8.5 Marketing and Promoting Your E-book

Marketing and promoting your e-book are essential steps to ensure its success. Effective strategies for launching, leveraging social media and email marketing, and utilizing book reviews and promotions can significantly boost your book's visibility and sales. This section provides comprehensive guidance on these aspects.

Strategies for Launching Your E-book

1. **Pre-Launch Preparation**:

- **Build Anticipation**: Start promoting your e-book weeks or even months before the launch. Use teasers, cover reveals, and sneak peeks to build excitement and anticipation among your audience.

- **Launch Team**: Assemble a launch team consisting of loyal readers, friends, and influencers. Provide them with advance copies of your e-book and encourage them to share their reviews and spread the word on social media.

- **Landing Page**: Create a dedicated landing page for your e-book. Include the book's cover, description, author bio, and a compelling call-to-action. Ensure the page is optimized for conversions.

2. **Launch Day Activities**:

- **Press Release**: Issue a press release announcing your e-book's launch. Distribute it through press release distribution services and send it directly to relevant media outlets, blogs, and influencers.

- **Social Media Blitz**: Conduct a social media blitz on launch day. Share engaging posts, images, and videos about your e-book across all your social media platforms. Use relevant hashtags to increase visibility.

- **Promotional Offers**: Offer special launch day promotions, such as limited-time discounts or bonus content for early buyers. These incentives can drive immediate sales and create buzz.

Using Social Media and Email Marketing

1. **Social Media Marketing**:

- **Platform Selection**: Focus on the social media platforms where your target audience is most active. Common platforms for book marketing include Facebook, Twitter, Instagram, and LinkedIn.

- **Content Strategy**: Develop a content strategy that includes a mix of promotional posts, engaging content related to your book's theme, and interactive posts that encourage audience participation. Use a social media calendar to plan and schedule your posts.

- **Engagement**: Engage with your followers by responding to comments, participating in discussions, and sharing user-generated content. Building a community around your book fosters loyalty and word-of-mouth promotion.

- **Paid Advertising**: Invest in paid social media advertising to reach a larger audience. Platforms like Facebook and Instagram offer targeted advertising options that can help you reach potential readers based on their interests, behaviors, and demographics.

2. **Email Marketing**:

- **Build Your List**: Start building your email list well before your e-book's launch. Offer a free resource, such as a sample chapter or a related e-book, in exchange for email sign-ups.

- **Segmentation**: Segment your email list based on factors such as interests, engagement level, and purchase history. This allows you to send targeted and personalized emails that resonate with your subscribers.

- **Launch Sequence**: Create a launch email sequence that includes pre-launch teasers, launch day announcements, and follow-up emails. Include clear calls-to-action and links to purchase your e-book.

- **Ongoing Engagement**: Maintain regular communication with your email list even after the launch. Share updates, new releases, exclusive content, and special offers to keep your audience engaged and interested in your work.

Leveraging Book Reviews and Promotions

1. **Book Reviews**:

   - **Advance Review Copies (ARCs)**: Send out ARCs to book bloggers, reviewers, and influencers in your niche. Encourage them to post honest reviews on platforms like Amazon, Goodreads, and their blogs.

   - **Review Request**: Include a polite request for reviews at the end of your e-book. Explain how reviews help other readers discover your book and provide a link to where they can leave a review.

   - **Review Platforms**: Submit your e-book to review platforms such as NetGalley and BookSirens. These platforms connect authors with readers who are willing to provide honest reviews in exchange for a free copy.

2. **Promotions and Giveaways**:

   - **Limited-Time Discounts**: Offer limited-time discounts to create a sense of urgency and boost sales. Platforms like Amazon KDP allow you to run Kindle Countdown Deals or temporarily lower the price of your e-book.

   - **Free Promotions**: Run free promotions to increase downloads and exposure. This strategy can be particularly effective if you have multiple books, as readers who enjoy the free book may purchase your other titles.

   - **Giveaways**: Host giveaways on social media or through your email list. Offer free copies of your e-book, signed copies, or related merchandise. Giveaways can generate excitement and attract new readers.

3. **Collaborations and Cross-Promotions**:

   - **Author Collaborations**: Collaborate with other authors in your genre for joint promotions, such as bundle deals or co-hosted webinars. This can expand your reach to each other's audiences.

- **Influencer Partnerships**: Partner with influencers who have a strong following in your niche. They can help promote your e-book through their platforms, reaching a broader audience.

- **Cross-Promotion**: Cross-promote your e-book with complementary products or services. For example, if your e-book is about fitness, partner with a fitness equipment brand to offer a joint promotion.

Example Table: Marketing and Promotion Strategies

Strategy	Actions	Benefits
Pre-Launch Preparation	Build anticipation, assemble a launch team, create a landing page	Increased awareness and excitement
Launch Day Activities	Issue press release, social media blitz, offer promotional deals	Immediate sales boost, media coverage
Social Media Marketing	Platform selection, content strategy, engagement, paid advertising	Broader reach, community building
Email Marketing	Build list, segmentation, launch sequence, ongoing engagement	Direct communication, higher conversion rates
Book Reviews	Send ARCs, request reviews, use review platforms	Enhanced credibility, increased visibility

Strategy	Actions	Benefits
Promotions and Giveaways	Limited-time discounts, free promotions, giveaways	Higher sales, increased downloads
Collaborations	Author collaborations, influencer partnerships, cross-promotion	Expanded reach, new audience acquisition

Effectively marketing and promoting your e-book requires a strategic approach that leverages various channels and tactics. By preparing for a successful launch, using social media and email marketing to engage with your audience, and leveraging book reviews and promotions, you can maximize your e-book's visibility and sales. These efforts will help you build a strong readership and establish your presence in the self-publishing market.

Chapter 9: Creating and Monetizing a YouTube Channel

9.1 Starting a YouTube Channel

Starting a YouTube channel can be a highly effective way to generate passive income. This section guides you through choosing a niche for your channel, setting up and optimizing your YouTube account, and planning your video content.

Choosing a Niche for Your Channel

1. **Identify Your Passion and Expertise**:

   - **Passion-Driven Content**: Select a niche that you are passionate about. Your enthusiasm will keep you motivated and engaged, making it easier to produce consistent content.

   - **Expertise**: Choose a niche where you have knowledge or expertise. This will establish you as an authority and help you provide valuable content to your audience.

2. **Research Market Demand**:

   - **Trending Topics**: Use tools like Google Trends, YouTube Trends, and social media platforms to identify trending topics within your areas of interest. Choose a niche with growing popularity to increase your chances of success.

   - **Keyword Research**: Conduct keyword research using tools like TubeBuddy, VidIQ, or the YouTube search bar. Identify popular search terms related to potential niches to gauge audience interest and search volume.

3. **Assess Competition**:

   - **Competitive Analysis**: Analyze existing channels in your potential niche. Study their content, viewership, engagement, and monetization strategies. Identify gaps or opportunities where you can offer something unique or improved.

- **Niche Size**: Consider the size of the niche. A highly competitive niche may be harder to break into, while a very small niche might not attract enough viewers. Aim for a balance where there is sufficient interest but manageable competition.

4. **Target Audience**:

- **Demographics**: Define the demographics of your target audience, including age, gender, location, and interests. Understanding your audience helps tailor your content to their preferences.

- **Engagement Potential**: Choose a niche that encourages high viewer engagement. Topics that spark discussions, questions, and community building tend to perform well on YouTube.

Setting Up and Optimizing Your YouTube Account

1. **Creating Your YouTube Account**:

- **Google Account**: Sign up for a Google account if you don't already have one. Use this account to create your YouTube channel.

- **Channel Name**: Choose a channel name that reflects your niche and is easy to remember. Ensure it aligns with your brand identity and resonates with your target audience.

2. **Channel Art and Branding**:

- **Profile Picture**: Upload a high-quality profile picture, such as a logo or professional photo. This image represents your brand across the platform.

- **Channel Banner**: Design an eye-catching channel banner that visually communicates your channel's theme and includes key information like your upload schedule or social media handles. Use tools like Canva or Adobe Spark for professional designs.

3. **Channel Description and Keywords**:

- **About Section**: Write a compelling channel description that clearly explains what your channel is about and what viewers can expect. Highlight your unique selling points and include relevant keywords to improve searchability.

- **Channel Keywords**: Add relevant keywords to your channel settings. These keywords help YouTube understand your content and improve your channel's visibility in search results.

4. **Channel Links and Contact Information**:

- **Social Media Links**: Add links to your social media profiles and website in your channel's About section. This helps build a connected online presence and directs traffic between platforms.

- **Contact Info**: Provide an email address for business inquiries. This makes it easy for potential collaborators and sponsors to reach you.

Planning Your Video Content

1. **Content Strategy**:

- **Content Pillars**: Identify 3-5 core content pillars that align with your niche. These are broad topics that you can consistently create content around, helping to establish your channel's identity and attract a loyal audience.

- **Video Formats**: Decide on the types of videos you will produce, such as tutorials, reviews, vlogs, interviews, or listicles. Varying your video formats can keep your content fresh and engaging.

2. **Content Calendar**:

- **Upload Schedule**: Establish a consistent upload schedule, whether it's weekly, bi-weekly, or monthly. Consistency helps retain viewers and improves your channel's performance in YouTube's algorithm.

- **Planning Ahead**: Create a content calendar to plan your videos in advance. This helps ensure a steady stream of content and allows you to prepare for key dates or events relevant to your niche.

3. **Video Topics and Titles**:

- **Brainstorming**: Generate a list of potential video topics based on your content pillars. Use keyword research to identify popular and relevant topics.

- **Compelling Titles**: Craft engaging and descriptive titles for your videos. Include keywords and phrases that viewers are likely to search for, and ensure the titles are intriguing enough to encourage clicks.

4. **Script and Structure**:

- **Scripting**: Write scripts or outlines for your videos to ensure clear and organized delivery. Scripting helps you stay on topic and convey your message effectively.

- **Video Structure**: Structure your videos with a clear beginning, middle, and end. Start with a strong hook to grab attention, present your main content in an engaging way, and conclude with a call-to-action (CTA) encouraging likes, comments, and subscriptions.

5. **SEO Optimization**:

- **Tags and Descriptions**: Use relevant tags and detailed descriptions for your videos. Tags help categorize your content, while descriptions provide additional context and keywords for YouTube's algorithm.

- **Thumbnails**: Design custom thumbnails that are visually appealing and accurately represent your video content. Thumbnails play a crucial role in attracting viewers and increasing click-through rates.

Example Table: Tools for YouTube Channel Setup and Optimization

Tool	Purpose	Features	Pricing
TubeBuddy	Channel Optimization	Keyword research, tags, SEO tools	Free, with paid plans
VidIQ	Channel Analytics and Optimization	Video analytics, keyword research, competitor analysis	Free, with paid plans
Canva	Graphic Design	Thumbnails, channel art, social media graphics	Free, with paid plans
Adobe Spark	Graphic Design	Thumbnails, channel art, social media graphics	Subscription-based
Google Trends	Market Research	Identifying trending topics and keywords	Free

Starting a YouTube channel involves careful planning and optimization. By choosing a well-researched niche, setting up and optimizing your account professionally, and planning engaging video content, you can build a successful channel that attracts viewers and generates passive income. Implementing these strategies will set a strong foundation for your YouTube journey and help you stand out in the competitive landscape.

9.2 Creating Engaging Video Content

Creating engaging video content is essential for attracting and retaining viewers on your YouTube channel. This section provides tips for filming and editing videos, crafting thumbnails and titles that attract viewers, and using YouTube SEO to increase visibility.

Tips for Filming and Editing Videos

1. **Filming Techniques**:

   - **Equipment**: Invest in a good quality camera and microphone. Clear visuals and crisp audio are crucial for a professional appearance. For beginners, modern smartphones can also produce high-quality videos.

   - **Lighting**: Ensure proper lighting. Natural light is often the best, but you can also use affordable ring lights or softboxes to achieve even lighting. Avoid harsh shadows and overexposure.

   - **Framing and Composition**: Follow basic composition rules like the rule of thirds to create visually appealing shots. Ensure the subject is well-framed and the background is not distracting.

   - **Steady Shots**: Use a tripod or stabilizer to avoid shaky footage. Smooth, steady shots make your videos more professional and easier to watch.

2. **Editing Tips**:

   - **Software**: Choose an editing software that fits your needs and skill level. Popular options include Adobe Premiere Pro, Final Cut Pro, and free alternatives like DaVinci Resolve.

   - **Cutting and Trimming**: Edit out unnecessary parts to keep your video concise and engaging. Aim for a good flow and pacing that keeps the viewer's attention.

- **Transitions and Effects**: Use transitions and effects sparingly. Overusing them can be distracting. Stick to clean cuts and simple transitions like fades or slides.

- **Sound and Music**: Balance your audio levels to ensure clarity. Add background music to enhance your videos, but ensure it doesn't overpower your voice. Use royalty-free music to avoid copyright issues.

- **Text and Graphics**: Incorporate text and graphics to highlight key points, add emphasis, or provide additional information. Ensure they are easy to read and complement the overall design.

Creating Thumbnails and Titles That Attract Viewers

1. **Thumbnails**:

- **Visual Appeal**: Thumbnails are the first thing viewers see. Create visually appealing thumbnails that accurately represent your content. Use bright colors, bold text, and high-contrast images to stand out.

- **Consistency**: Maintain a consistent style for your thumbnails to create a cohesive brand. Use similar fonts, colors, and layouts across your videos.

- **Faces and Expressions**: Thumbnails with faces and expressive emotions tend to attract more clicks. If relevant, include your face or the faces of people in your video.

- **Text Overlay**: Add a short, compelling text overlay that highlights the main topic or benefit of your video. Keep it concise and readable even on small screens.

2. **Titles**:

- **Keyword Optimization**: Use relevant keywords in your titles to improve searchability. Tools like TubeBuddy and VidIQ can help identify high-performing keywords.

- **Clarity and Intrigue**: Craft clear and intriguing titles that accurately describe the content. Avoid clickbait, but aim to pique curiosity. For example, "10 Tips for Better Video Editing" is clear and informative.

- **Length**: Keep your titles concise and to the point. Ideally, titles should be between 60-70 characters to ensure they are not cut off in search results.

- **Consistency with Content**: Ensure your title aligns with the content of your video. Misleading titles can frustrate viewers and harm your channel's credibility.

Using YouTube SEO to Increase Visibility

1. **Keyword Research**:

- **Identify Keywords**: Use tools like Google Trends, YouTube Search Suggest, TubeBuddy, and VidIQ to identify relevant keywords for your niche. Look for keywords with high search volume and moderate competition.

- **Long-Tail Keywords**: Focus on long-tail keywords (e.g., "beginner video editing tips") that are specific and less competitive. These can help you rank higher in search results.

2. **Optimizing Video Elements**:

- **Title**: Incorporate primary keywords naturally into your video title. Ensure the title is engaging and accurately reflects the content.

- **Description**: Write a detailed and keyword-rich description. Include your primary and secondary keywords naturally within the first few lines. Provide a brief overview of the video, key points, and any relevant links.

- **Tags**: Add relevant tags to your video. Use a mix of broad and specific tags that relate to your content. Tags help

YouTube understand the context of your video and improve its discoverability.

- **Closed Captions and Subtitles**: Adding closed captions and subtitles can improve accessibility and SEO. YouTube's algorithm can index the text in your captions, making your content more discoverable.

3. **Engagement Metrics**:

- **Watch Time**: Encourage viewers to watch your videos longer. Higher watch time signals to YouTube that your content is valuable, which can improve your ranking.

- **Likes, Comments, and Shares**: Engage with your audience by encouraging likes, comments, and shares. Respond to comments to build community and increase engagement.

- **Click-Through Rate (CTR)**: Monitor your video's CTR. A high CTR indicates that your thumbnail and title are effective. Experiment with different thumbnail designs and titles to optimize CTR.

4. **Playlists and End Screens**:

- **Playlists**: Organize your videos into playlists to increase watch time. Playlists keep viewers on your channel longer by automatically playing related content.

- **End Screens**: Use end screens to promote other videos, playlists, or encourage subscriptions. End screens appear in the last 20 seconds of your video and can drive additional engagement.

Example Table: Tools for Creating and Optimizing Video Content

Tool	Purpose	Features	Pricing
Adobe Premiere Pro	Video Editing	Advanced editing tools, effects, and transitions	Subscription-based
Final Cut Pro	Video Editing	Professional editing features, easy integration with Mac	One-time purchase
TubeBuddy	YouTube SEO and Analytics	Keyword research, tag suggestions, analytics	Free, with paid plans
VidIQ	YouTube SEO and Analytics	Keyword research, competitor analysis, video score	Free, with paid plans
Canva	Thumbnail and Graphic Design	Easy-to-use design tools, templates for thumbnails	Free, with paid plans
DaVinci Resolve	Video Editing	Professional-grade editing, color correction, free version available	Free, with paid plans
Epidemic Sound	Music and Sound Effects	Royalty-free music and sound effects	Subscription-based

Creating engaging video content requires a combination of effective filming and editing techniques, eye-catching thumbnails and titles, and strategic YouTube SEO practices. By implementing these strategies, you can increase your video's visibility, attract more viewers, and build a successful YouTube channel that generates passive income.

9.3 Monetizing Your YouTube Channel

Monetizing your YouTube channel is a crucial step towards generating passive income from your content. This section explores joining the YouTube Partner Program, using AdSense and other ad networks, and exploring sponsorships and brand deals to maximize your revenue.

Joining the YouTube Partner Program

1. **Eligibility Requirements**:

   - **Subscriber Count**: You need at least 1,000 subscribers to be eligible for the YouTube Partner Program (YPP).

   - **Watch Hours**: Your channel must have accrued 4,000 watch hours in the past 12 months.

   - **Content Guidelines**: Ensure your content complies with YouTube's Community Guidelines and Terms of Service. Channels with repeated violations may be denied or removed from the program.

   - **AdSense Account**: You must have an AdSense account linked to your YouTube channel to receive payments.

2. **Application Process**:

   - **Review Guidelines**: Before applying, review the YouTube Partner Program policies and monetization policies.

   - **Apply for YPP**: Go to the Monetization tab in your YouTube Studio and follow the steps to apply. This includes agreeing to the YPP terms, signing up for AdSense, and setting up your preferences.

- **Channel Review**: Once you apply, YouTube will review your channel to ensure it meets the eligibility and policy requirements. This process can take several weeks.

3. **Monetization Features**:

- **Ad Revenue**: Once approved, you can earn revenue from ads displayed on your videos. Ad formats include display ads, overlay ads, skippable video ads, non-skippable video ads, and bumper ads.

- **Channel Memberships**: Offer channel memberships to your viewers for a monthly fee. Members gain access to exclusive perks like badges, emojis, and members-only content.

- **Super Chat and Super Stickers**: Enable these features during live streams, allowing viewers to purchase highlighted messages and stickers to show their support.

- **Merchandise Shelf**: Promote your merchandise directly on your YouTube channel through the merchandise shelf feature, available if you have a merch store linked to YouTube.

Using AdSense and Other Ad Networks

1. **AdSense Integration**:

- **Setting Up AdSense**: Link your AdSense account to your YouTube channel during the YPP application process. Ensure your AdSense account is correctly set up with accurate payment information.

- **Ad Types**: AdSense serves various ad types on your videos. Experiment with different ad formats and placements to optimize your earnings.

2. **Optimizing Ad Revenue**:

- **Content Strategy**: Create content that attracts high viewer engagement and retention. Longer watch times can lead to more ad impressions and higher revenue.

- **Ad Placement**: Strategically place ads in your videos. For videos longer than 10 minutes, you can insert mid-roll ads. Avoid overloading your videos with ads, which can deter viewers.

- **Analytics**: Use YouTube Analytics to track your ad performance. Monitor metrics like CPM (cost per thousand impressions), click-through rate (CTR), and audience demographics to refine your strategy.

3. **Exploring Other Ad Networks**:

- **Ad Networks for Additional Revenue**: Consider integrating other ad networks like Media.net or Amazon Associates to diversify your income streams. These networks offer various ad formats, including contextual ads and affiliate links.

- **Affiliate Marketing**: Promote affiliate products in your videos and earn a commission for each sale made through your affiliate links. Ensure the products are relevant to your audience and provide value.

Exploring Sponsorships and Brand Deals

1. **Finding Sponsorship Opportunities**:

- **Brand Outreach**: Proactively reach out to brands that align with your niche and audience. Craft a professional pitch highlighting your channel's value, audience demographics, and engagement metrics.

- **Influencer Platforms**: Sign up on influencer marketing platforms like FameBit, Grapevine, and Social Bluebook. These platforms connect creators with brands looking for sponsorship opportunities.

2. **Negotiating Deals**:

- **Value Proposition**: Clearly articulate your value proposition to potential sponsors. Highlight your audience size, engagement rates, and the unique aspects of your channel that make it an ideal fit for their brand.

- **Pricing**: Determine your pricing based on factors like your subscriber count, average views per video, engagement rate, and the scope of the sponsorship. Be transparent about your rates and flexible in negotiations.

3. **Delivering Sponsored Content**:

- **Authenticity**: Ensure sponsored content aligns with your brand and provides value to your audience. Authenticity is key to maintaining trust and credibility.

- **Disclosure**: Comply with legal requirements by disclosing sponsored content. Use YouTube's built-in disclosure tools and verbally acknowledge sponsorships in your videos.

- **Performance Tracking**: Monitor the performance of your sponsored content. Provide brands with detailed reports on metrics like views, engagement, and conversions to build long-term partnerships.

Example Table: Monetization Methods Comparison

Monetization Method	Description	Revenue Potential	Key Considerations
YouTube Partner Program	Earn ad revenue, channel memberships, Super Chat, and merchandise	High, with large audience	Requires 1,000 subscribers and 4,000 watch hours

Monetization Method	Description	Revenue Potential	Key Considerations
AdSense	Integrate AdSense for ad revenue	Moderate to High	Optimize ad placements and content strategy
Other Ad Networks	Use additional ad networks like Media.net and Amazon Associates	Moderate	Diversify income, ensure relevance to content
Sponsorships	Partner with brands for sponsored content	High, if well-negotiated	Authenticity, compliance with disclosure regulations
Affiliate Marketing	Promote products and earn commission on sales	Variable	Product relevance, trustworthiness of recommendations

Monetizing your YouTube channel involves multiple strategies to maximize your income. Joining the YouTube Partner Program, using AdSense and other ad networks, and exploring sponsorships and brand deals are all effective ways to generate revenue. By diversifying your income streams and optimizing each method, you can build a sustainable and profitable YouTube channel.

9.4 Growing Your YouTube Audience

Building a large and engaged audience on YouTube is essential for the success of your channel. This section explores strategies for increasing subscribers and views, engaging with your audience through comments and community posts, and collaborating with other YouTubers.

Strategies for Increasing Subscribers and Views

1. **Consistent Content Schedule**:

- **Regular Uploads**: Develop a consistent upload schedule to keep your audience engaged and coming back for more. Whether it's weekly, bi-weekly, or monthly, stick to your schedule to build viewer trust and loyalty.

- **Content Planning**: Plan your content in advance to ensure a steady stream of videos. Use a content calendar to organize your topics and avoid last-minute rushes.

2. **High-Quality Content**:

- **Value-Driven Videos**: Create content that provides value to your audience, whether through education, entertainment, or inspiration. High-quality, valuable content is more likely to be shared and recommended.

- **Production Quality**: Invest in good equipment for filming and editing. Clear audio, sharp visuals, and professional editing can significantly enhance viewer experience and retention.

3. **SEO Optimization**:

- **Keyword Research**: Use tools like TubeBuddy, VidIQ, and Google Trends to identify relevant keywords. Incorporate these keywords into your video titles, descriptions, and tags.

- **Thumbnails and Titles**: Create eye-catching thumbnails and compelling titles that incorporate keywords. Effective thumbnails and titles can greatly improve your click-through rate (CTR).

4. **Engaging Introductions**:

   - **Strong Hooks**: Start your videos with a strong hook to grab the viewer's attention within the first few seconds. Outline what viewers can expect and why they should keep watching.

   - **Concise Intros**: Keep your introductions concise and to the point. Quickly get to the main content to maintain viewer interest.

5. **Calls to Action**:

   - **Subscribe Prompts**: Include clear calls to action (CTAs) asking viewers to subscribe to your channel. Place these CTAs strategically within the video, such as at the beginning, middle, and end.

   - **Engagement Encouragement**: Encourage viewers to like, comment, and share your videos. Engaged viewers are more likely to become loyal subscribers.

Engaging with Your Audience through Comments and Community Posts

1. **Active Comment Section**:

   - **Respond to Comments**: Actively respond to comments on your videos. Engaging with your viewers shows that you value their feedback and helps build a community around your channel.

   - **Foster Discussions**: Encourage discussions by asking questions and prompting viewers to share their thoughts. Engaging comment sections can boost your video's visibility and engagement metrics.

2. **Community Posts**:

   - **YouTube Community Tab**: Utilize the Community tab to post updates, polls, and behind-the-scenes content. This feature allows you to engage with your audience outside of video uploads.

- **Interactive Posts**: Use polls and questions to gather viewer feedback and involve them in your content creation process. Interactive posts can increase engagement and make viewers feel more connected to your channel.

3. **Viewer Acknowledgment**:

- **Shout-Outs**: Give shout-outs to loyal viewers and top commenters in your videos. Recognizing your audience can boost loyalty and encourage more engagement.

- **Feedback Implementation**: Show your audience that you value their input by implementing their suggestions and ideas. Acknowledging feedback and making improvements based on viewer input can enhance viewer satisfaction and loyalty.

Collaborating with Other YouTubers

1. **Identifying Potential Collaborators**:

- **Niche Relevance**: Look for YouTubers within your niche or related niches. Collaborations are more effective when both channels share a similar target audience.

- **Audience Size and Engagement**: Consider the audience size and engagement levels of potential collaborators. Collaborate with channels that have an engaged audience, even if their subscriber count is smaller than yours.

2. **Types of Collaborations**:

- **Guest Appearances**: Feature each other in your videos as guest appearances. This introduces your content to each other's audiences and can drive cross-channel traffic.

- **Collab Series**: Create a collaboration series where you and another YouTuber produce a series of videos together. This can keep viewers engaged over multiple videos and channels.

- **Joint Projects**: Work on joint projects or challenges that span across both channels. Joint projects can create buzz and attract viewers from both audiences.

3. **Promoting Collaborations**:

- **Cross-Promotion**: Promote the collaboration on both channels and social media platforms. Use teasers and behind-the-scenes content to build anticipation.
- **End Screens and Cards**: Use YouTube's end screens and cards to link to your collaborator's channel or video. This encourages viewers to check out the other channel.

Example Table: Strategies for Growing YouTube Audience

Strategy	Actions	Benefits
Consistent Content Schedule	Develop and stick to a regular upload schedule	Builds viewer trust and loyalty
High-Quality Content	Invest in good equipment, provide valuable content	Enhances viewer experience, increases shares
SEO Optimization	Use keyword research tools, optimize titles and descriptions	Improves search visibility, increases views
Engaging Introductions	Start with a strong hook, keep intros concise	Retains viewer interest from the start
Calls to Action	Ask viewers to subscribe, like, comment, and share	Increases engagement and subscriber count

Strategy	Actions	Benefits
Active Comment Section	Respond to comments, encourage discussions	Builds community, boosts engagement metrics
Community Posts	Use polls, updates, and interactive content in the Community tab	Keeps audience engaged between video uploads
Viewer Acknowledgment	Give shout-outs, implement viewer feedback	Enhances viewer loyalty and satisfaction
Collaborations	Feature guest appearances, create collab series, joint projects	Expands reach, introduces new audiences
Promoting Collaborations	Cross-promote on both channels, use end screens and cards	Drives cross-channel traffic

Growing your YouTube audience requires a strategic approach that combines consistent content creation, active audience engagement, and collaborative efforts with other YouTubers. By implementing these strategies, you can build a loyal and engaged subscriber base, increase your views, and enhance your channel's overall success.

9.5 Diversifying Your YouTube Income

Diversifying your income streams on YouTube is crucial for building a sustainable and profitable channel. This section covers creating merchandise and digital products, using Patreon and crowdfunding, and expanding to other platforms like Twitch and TikTok.

Creating Merchandise and Digital Products

1. **Merchandise**:

   - **Product Selection**: Choose products that resonate with your audience and reflect your brand. Popular merchandise items include t-shirts, hoodies, mugs, and stickers.

   - **Design**: Create unique and appealing designs that your audience will want to purchase. Use tools like Adobe Illustrator or Canva, or hire a professional designer.

   - **Print-on-Demand Services**: Utilize print-on-demand services like Teespring, Merch by Amazon, or Printful. These platforms handle production, shipping, and customer service, allowing you to focus on promotion.

   - **Promotion**: Promote your merchandise in your videos, descriptions, and social media channels. Use calls to action and showcase the products in use.

2. **Digital Products**:

   - **E-books and Guides**: Create e-books or guides on topics relevant to your channel. These could be in-depth tutorials, how-to guides, or collections of tips and tricks.

   - **Courses and Webinars**: Develop online courses or webinars. Platforms like Udemy, Teachable, and Skillshare allow you to host and sell your courses to a broad audience.

   - **Templates and Tools**: If you have expertise in design or content creation, offer templates, presets, or other digital tools that your audience can use.

3. **Selling Platforms**:

   - **Website Integration**: Use e-commerce platforms like Shopify or WooCommerce to sell merchandise and digital products directly from your website.

- **YouTube Merch Shelf**: If you're eligible, use YouTube's Merch Shelf feature to display and sell your merchandise directly under your videos.

Using Patreon and Crowdfunding

1. **Patreon**:

- **Setting Up**: Create a Patreon page where fans can support you through monthly subscriptions. Offer different tier levels with varying perks and benefits.

- **Exclusive Content**: Provide exclusive content to your patrons, such as behind-the-scenes videos, early access to new content, or personalized shout-outs.

- **Community Engagement**: Use Patreon to build a closer community with your most dedicated fans. Engage with them through posts, messages, and live streams.

2. **Crowdfunding**:

- **Campaign Platforms**: Use platforms like Kickstarter or Indiegogo to fund specific projects. Whether you're producing a high-budget video series, launching a new product, or planning a special event, crowdfunding can provide the necessary financial support.

- **Campaign Strategy**: Clearly outline your project's goals, timeline, and budget. Offer compelling rewards and incentives for different levels of support.

- **Promotion**: Promote your crowdfunding campaign through your YouTube channel, social media, email lists, and collaborations with other creators.

Expanding to Other Platforms (Twitch, TikTok)

1. **Twitch**:

- **Streaming Content**: Use Twitch for live streaming content that complements your YouTube videos. This could include gaming, Q&A sessions, live tutorials, or behind-the-scenes looks at your creative process.

- **Monetization Options**: Twitch offers various monetization options, including subscriptions, Bits (a virtual good that viewers can purchase to cheer during streams), and ad revenue.

- **Engagement**: Engage with your Twitch audience in real-time through chat. Building a community on Twitch can increase your overall brand loyalty and viewership.

2. **TikTok**:

- **Short-Form Content**: Leverage TikTok's platform for short-form content to reach a broader audience. Create entertaining, informative, or viral videos that align with your YouTube content.

- **Cross-Promotion**: Use TikTok to promote your YouTube channel. Include links to your YouTube videos in your TikTok profile and encourage viewers to check out your longer content.

- **Monetization**: TikTok offers monetization through its Creator Fund, brand partnerships, and sponsored content. Engage with trends and use popular hashtags to increase your visibility.

3. **Other Platforms**:

- **Instagram and Facebook**: Share content snippets, behind-the-scenes posts, and engage with your audience on Instagram and Facebook. These platforms also offer monetization opportunities through branded content and ads.

- **Podcasting**: Start a podcast to explore topics in-depth. Use platforms like Anchor to distribute your podcast and monetize through sponsorships and listener support.

Example Table: Diversifying Income Streams

Income Stream	Description	Platform Examples	Key Benefits
Merchandise	Selling branded products like t-shirts, mugs, and stickers	Teespring, Merch by Amazon, Printful	Passive income, brand promotion
Digital Products	E-books, online courses, templates	Udemy, Teachable, Shopify	Scalable, low overhead costs
Patreon	Monthly subscriptions for exclusive content	Patreon	Recurring revenue, community building
Crowdfunding	Funding specific projects through supporter contributions	Kickstarter, Indiegogo	Funding for large projects, audience engagement
Twitch Streaming	Live streaming content with viewer interaction	Twitch	Real-time engagement, multiple revenue streams
TikTok	Short-form video content for broader audience reach	TikTok	Viral potential, cross-promotion
Other Social Media	Content sharing and engagement	Instagram, Facebook	Increased visibility,

Income Stream	Description	Platform Examples	Key Benefits
	on platforms like Instagram		additional ad revenue
Podcasting	In-depth audio content on various topics	Anchor, Spotify	Diversified content, sponsorship opportunities

Diversifying your income streams on YouTube involves leveraging multiple platforms and revenue models. By creating merchandise and digital products, using Patreon and crowdfunding, and expanding to other platforms like Twitch and TikTok, you can build a robust and sustainable income strategy. This approach not only maximizes your earning potential but also increases your reach and strengthens your brand across different mediums.

Chapter 10: Building a Passive Income Mindset

10.1 The Importance of Mindset in Passive Income Success

Achieving success in building passive income streams is not just about having the right strategies and tools; it's equally about cultivating the right mindset. Your mindset influences your actions, perseverance, and ultimately, your success. This section explores how mindset impacts passive income success, identifies common mental barriers and ways to overcome them, and provides guidance on developing a growth mindset.

How Mindset Influences Your Success in Building Passive Income

1. **Belief in Possibility**:

- **Self-Efficacy**: Believing in your ability to create and manage passive income streams is fundamental. Self-efficacy affects how you approach challenges, set goals, and persevere in the face of obstacles. Those with high self-efficacy are more likely to take initiative and persist through difficulties.

- **Positive Expectations**: Maintaining a positive outlook on your passive income journey can significantly impact your results. Expecting success can lead to taking proactive steps, whereas expecting failure can result in self-sabotage and lack of effort.

2. **Resilience and Persistence**:

- **Long-Term Vision**: Building passive income often requires a long-term commitment. A mindset that embraces delayed gratification and long-term planning is essential.

Recognize that building sustainable income streams takes time and persistence.

- **Handling Setbacks**: The journey to passive income success is rarely smooth. A resilient mindset helps you bounce back from setbacks, learn from failures, and continue moving forward. View challenges as opportunities for growth rather than insurmountable obstacles.

3. **Openness to Learning**:

- **Continuous Improvement**: A mindset open to learning and growth is crucial. Stay curious and continually seek knowledge about new strategies, tools, and trends in passive income generation. This proactive approach helps you adapt and improve your methods over time.

- **Adaptability**: The financial landscape and opportunities for passive income are constantly evolving. Being adaptable and open to change allows you to pivot when necessary and take advantage of new opportunities.

Common Mental Barriers and How to Overcome Them

1. **Fear of Failure**:

- **Understanding Failure**: Recognize that failure is a natural part of any entrepreneurial journey. It provides valuable lessons and insights that can lead to future success. Reframe failure as a learning experience rather than a definitive end.

- **Action Steps**: Start with small, manageable projects to build confidence and experience. Gradually take on larger challenges as your skills and confidence grow.

2. **Procrastination**:

- **Identifying Causes**: Procrastination often stems from fear, uncertainty, or overwhelm. Identify the root cause of your procrastination and address it directly.

- **Breaking Tasks Down**: Divide larger tasks into smaller, actionable steps. This makes the process less daunting and helps you maintain momentum. Use tools like to-do lists and time management apps to stay organized and on track.

3. **Perfectionism**:

- **Embracing Imperfection**: Understand that perfectionism can hinder progress. Aim for progress rather than perfection. Accept that mistakes and imperfections are part of the learning process.

- **Setting Realistic Goals**: Set achievable goals and deadlines. Recognize that done is better than perfect, and continuous improvement is more valuable than striving for flawlessness.

Developing a Growth Mindset

1. **What is a Growth Mindset?**:

- **Definition**: Coined by psychologist Carol Dweck, a growth mindset is the belief that abilities and intelligence can be developed through dedication and hard work. This contrasts with a fixed mindset, where individuals believe their abilities are static and unchangeable.

- **Benefits**: A growth mindset fosters resilience, a love for learning, and a willingness to embrace challenges. It encourages you to see effort as a path to mastery and setbacks as opportunities for growth.

2. **Cultivating a Growth Mindset**:

- **Embrace Challenges**: View challenges as opportunities to learn and grow. Instead of avoiding difficult tasks, face them head-on and persist through obstacles.

- **Learn from Criticism**: Accept constructive criticism as valuable feedback. Use it to improve your skills and strategies. Seek out mentors and peers who can provide insightful feedback.

- **Celebrate Effort and Progress**: Focus on the effort you put in and the progress you make, rather than just the end results. Celebrate small wins and milestones to stay motivated and build confidence.

3. **Practical Strategies**:

- **Journaling**: Keep a journal to reflect on your experiences, challenges, and growth. Documenting your journey helps you recognize patterns, celebrate progress, and learn from setbacks.

- **Affirmations**: Use positive affirmations to reinforce a growth mindset. Statements like "I can learn and improve" or "Every challenge is an opportunity to grow" can shift your mindset towards growth and resilience.

- **Surround Yourself with Positivity**: Engage with people who have a growth mindset and support your goals. Positive influences can reinforce your own growth mindset and provide encouragement during tough times.

Example Table: Fixed Mindset vs. Growth Mindset

Aspect	Fixed Mindset	Growth Mindset
Beliefs	Abilities are static and unchangeable	Abilities can be developed through effort
Challenges	Avoids challenges to avoid failure	Embraces challenges as opportunities to learn
Effort	Sees effort as fruitless or indicative of low ability	Sees effort as a path to mastery
Setbacks	Gets discouraged by setbacks	Uses setbacks as learning opportunities

Aspect	Fixed Mindset	Growth Mindset
Criticism	Ignores or deflects constructive criticism	Learns from criticism and uses it to improve
Success of Others	Feels threatened by others' success	Finds inspiration and lessons in others' success

Adopting the right mindset is fundamental to achieving success in building passive income. By understanding how your mindset influences your actions, overcoming common mental barriers, and developing a growth mindset, you can navigate the challenges of creating sustainable passive income streams with resilience and determination. This mental foundation will support your efforts and enhance your ability to achieve long-term financial independence.

10.2 Setting Realistic Expectations

When embarking on the journey to build passive income, it's essential to set realistic expectations. Understanding the timeline for achieving your goals, avoiding get-rich-quick schemes, and focusing on sustainable, long-term growth are crucial for long-term success and financial stability.

Understanding the Timeline for Building Passive Income

1. **Initial Investment and Effort**:
   - **Time and Effort**: Building passive income streams requires a significant initial investment of time and effort. Whether you are creating content for a blog, developing a course, investing in real estate, or setting up an e-commerce store, expect to spend considerable time upfront to set everything up.

- **Financial Investment**: Some passive income streams, like real estate or dividend investing, require financial investment. Understanding your financial commitments and planning accordingly is critical.

2. **Gradual Growth**:

- **Slow Start**: Passive income streams often start small and grow gradually. It may take months or even years to see substantial income. Patience is essential during this period.
- **Compounding Effect**: Over time, the efforts you put in initially can compound. For example, a blog may start earning small amounts from ads, but as traffic increases, so does the ad revenue. Similarly, investments grow through compounding interest and reinvested dividends.

3. **Setting Milestones**:

- **Short-Term Goals**: Establish short-term goals to keep yourself motivated. These could be monthly revenue targets, traffic milestones, or content creation goals.
- **Long-Term Vision**: Keep a long-term vision in mind. Understand that significant passive income will take time to build but is achievable with consistent effort and strategic planning.

Avoiding Get-Rich-Quick Schemes

1. **Recognizing Red Flags**:

- **Unrealistic Promises**: Be wary of schemes that promise quick and easy wealth with little effort. If something sounds too good to be true, it likely is.
- **Lack of Transparency**: Avoid opportunities that lack transparency. Legitimate business opportunities will provide clear information about the risks and rewards involved.

2. **Due Diligence**:

- **Research**: Conduct thorough research before committing to any passive income opportunity. Look for reviews, case studies, and testimonials from other users.
- **Expert Advice**: Consult with financial advisors or experts in the field. They can provide valuable insights and help you avoid scams.

3. **Sustainable Strategies**:

- **Focus on Proven Methods**: Concentrate on passive income strategies with a proven track record, such as real estate investing, stock market investments, or creating digital products.
- **Diversification**: Diversify your income streams to mitigate risk. Relying on a single source can be risky if it fails or becomes less profitable.

Focusing on Sustainable, Long-Term Growth

1. **Building a Solid Foundation**:

- **Education and Skill Development**: Invest time in learning and developing the skills necessary for your chosen passive income stream. For example, learning about SEO for blogging or understanding market trends for investing.
- **Quality Over Quantity**: Focus on producing high-quality content or products that provide real value. High-quality offerings attract more customers and sustain growth over time.

2. **Consistent Effort and Improvement**:

- **Regular Updates**: Continuously update and improve your offerings. For example, a blog should have regular new posts, and an online course should be updated with the latest information.

- **Feedback Loop**: Listen to feedback from your audience or customers. Use it to make improvements and enhance the value you provide.

3. **Monitoring and Adapting**:

- **Track Progress**: Use analytics and tracking tools to monitor the performance of your passive income streams. Understand what works and what doesn't.

- **Adapt Strategies**: Be flexible and willing to adapt your strategies based on performance data and market changes. The ability to pivot when necessary can keep your income streams healthy and growing.

Example Timeline: Building a Passive Income Stream

Timeframe	Activity	Expected Outcomes
Months 1-3	Research and initial setup	Basic infrastructure in place, initial content created
Months 3-6	Consistent content creation, initial promotion	Slow growth in traffic or user base
Months 6-12	Continued content creation, optimization	Increased traffic, small but steady income
Year 1-2	Scaling efforts, diversifying content/products	Noticeable increase in revenue, expanding audience
Year 2-5	Refinement and scaling, exploring new streams	Significant income, diversified passive income sources

Case Study: Sustainable Growth Example

Consider the example of Jane, who started a blog on personal finance. In the first few months, she focused on creating high-quality, valuable content and optimizing her site for search engines. Her initial traffic was modest, but she remained consistent with her content creation and marketing efforts.

By the end of the first year, her blog started to attract more visitors, and she monetized through ad networks and affiliate marketing. Over the next few years, she diversified her income by creating an online course and writing an e-book. Her patient and consistent efforts paid off, and by the fifth year, Jane's blog generated significant passive income, allowing her to focus on new ventures.

Setting realistic expectations is essential for anyone looking to build passive income. Understand the timeline involved, steer clear of get-rich-quick schemes, and focus on sustainable, long-term growth. With patience, persistence, and a strategic approach, achieving substantial passive income is within reach.

10.3 Staying Motivated and Persistent

Achieving success in building passive income streams requires not only strategic planning and execution but also a strong sense of motivation and persistence. This section explores strategies for maintaining motivation, overcoming setbacks and challenges, and celebrating small wins and progress.

Strategies for Maintaining Motivation

1. **Setting Clear Goals**:

   - **SMART Goals**: Set Specific, Measurable, Achievable, Relevant, and Time-bound (SMART) goals. Clear goals provide direction and a sense of purpose, making it easier to stay motivated.

- **Short-Term and Long-Term Goals**: Break down long-term goals into smaller, manageable short-term goals. Achieving these smaller milestones can provide immediate satisfaction and keep you motivated.

2. **Creating a Vision Board**:

- **Visual Representation**: Create a vision board that visually represents your goals and dreams. Include images, quotes, and other elements that inspire and remind you of what you are working towards.

- **Daily Visualization**: Spend a few minutes each day visualizing your success. This practice can reinforce your commitment and keep your goals at the forefront of your mind.

3. **Building a Support Network**:

- **Accountability Partners**: Find an accountability partner or join a group of like-minded individuals. Sharing your goals and progress with others can provide motivation and support.

- **Mentorship**: Seek out mentors who have achieved the success you aspire to. Their guidance and advice can help you stay on track and motivated.

4. **Routine and Discipline**:

- **Daily Habits**: Establish daily habits that contribute to your passive income goals. Consistent actions, even small ones, can lead to significant progress over time.

- **Time Management**: Allocate specific time blocks for working on your passive income projects. Creating a structured schedule helps maintain focus and productivity.

Overcoming Setbacks and Challenges

1. **Resilience Building**:

- **Positive Mindset**: Cultivate a positive mindset that views setbacks as opportunities to learn and grow. Remind yourself that challenges are part of the journey and can lead to valuable insights.

- **Stress Management**: Practice stress management techniques such as meditation, exercise, and deep breathing. Managing stress effectively can help you stay resilient in the face of difficulties.

2. **Problem-Solving Skills**:

- **Identify the Root Cause**: When facing a setback, take the time to identify the root cause. Understanding the underlying issues can help you develop effective solutions.

- **Brainstorm Solutions**: Generate multiple potential solutions and evaluate their pros and cons. Experiment with different approaches to find what works best.

3. **Seeking Support**:

- **Professional Help**: Don't hesitate to seek professional help when needed. Business coaches, financial advisors, or mental health professionals can provide valuable support and guidance.

- **Community Resources**: Leverage online forums, social media groups, and local meetups to connect with others who can offer advice and support.

Celebrating Small Wins and Progress

1. **Recognizing Achievements**:

- **Track Progress**: Keep a journal or use a tracking tool to record your progress. Documenting your achievements, no matter how small, can provide a sense of accomplishment and motivation.

- **Reflect on Milestones**: Regularly reflect on the milestones you have reached. Acknowledging how far you've come can boost your confidence and motivation.

2. **Rewarding Yourself**:

- **Set Rewards**: Establish rewards for achieving specific milestones. These can be simple pleasures like a favorite meal, a day off, or a small purchase. Rewards can serve as motivation to reach the next goal.
- **Celebrate Successes**: Celebrate your successes with friends and family. Sharing your achievements with others can enhance the sense of accomplishment and provide additional motivation.

3. **Continuous Learning and Improvement**:

- **Feedback Loop**: Regularly seek feedback on your progress and use it to make improvements. Continuous learning and adaptation can keep you engaged and motivated.
- **Educational Goals**: Set goals related to learning new skills or gaining knowledge that can help you achieve your passive income objectives. Investing in your personal and professional growth can lead to long-term success.

Example Table: Strategies for Staying Motivated and Persistent

Strategy	Description	Benefits
Setting Clear Goals	Establish SMART goals, break down long-term goals into short-term	Provides direction and sense of purpose
Creating a Vision Board	Visualize success through images,	Keeps goals at the forefront of your mind

Strategy	Description	Benefits
	quotes, and daily visualization	
Building a Support Network	Find accountability partners, join groups, seek mentorship	Offers motivation, guidance, and support
Routine and Discipline	Establish daily habits and structured schedules	Maintains focus and productivity
Resilience Building	Cultivate a positive mindset, practice stress management	Enhances ability to handle setbacks
Problem-Solving Skills	Identify root causes, brainstorm solutions	Develops effective strategies to overcome challenges
Seeking Support	Access professional help and community resources	Provides valuable advice and emotional support
Recognizing Achievements	Track progress, reflect on milestones	Boosts confidence and motivation
Rewarding Yourself	Set rewards for milestones, celebrate with others	Enhances sense of accomplishment
Continuous Learning and Improvement	Seek feedback, set educational goals	Promotes ongoing personal and professional growth

Staying motivated and persistent is essential for success in building passive income. By setting clear goals, building a support network, overcoming setbacks, and celebrating progress, you can maintain the drive and resilience needed to achieve your financial goals. These strategies will help you navigate the challenges and stay committed to your journey toward financial independence.

10.4 Continuous Learning and Adaptation

Success in building passive income streams hinges on the ability to stay informed, learn from others, and adapt strategies as needed. This section discusses the importance of continuous learning, the value of learning from successful passive income earners, and the necessity of adapting your strategies to stay relevant and effective.

The Importance of Staying Informed About New Opportunities

1. **Evolving Market Dynamics**:
   - **Changing Trends**: The market for passive income opportunities is dynamic. New trends and technologies can create fresh opportunities while making some strategies obsolete. Staying informed helps you leverage emerging trends and technologies.
   - **Regular Updates**: Follow industry news, subscribe to relevant blogs, and participate in forums to keep up with the latest developments. Platforms like Reddit, Medium, and specialized financial websites can be valuable resources.

2. **Educational Resources**:
   - **Books and Articles**: Invest time in reading books and articles on passive income strategies. Authors like Robert Kiyosaki and Tim Ferriss provide valuable insights into creating and managing passive income.
   - **Online Courses and Webinars**: Enroll in online courses and attend webinars on topics related to your passive

income streams. Websites like Udemy, Coursera, and LinkedIn Learning offer courses on a wide range of subjects.

3. **Networking and Communities**:

- **Professional Networks**: Join professional networks and associations related to your field. These networks can provide access to exclusive resources, industry reports, and networking opportunities.

- **Social Media Groups**: Participate in social media groups and forums where passive income strategies are discussed. Engaging with like-minded individuals can provide new perspectives and ideas.

Learning from Successful Passive Income Earners

1. **Case Studies and Success Stories**:

- **Inspiration and Insight**: Analyzing case studies and success stories of individuals who have successfully built passive income streams can provide inspiration and practical insights. Learn about their journeys, strategies, and challenges.

- **Best Practices**: Identify common best practices used by successful passive income earners. These practices can serve as a blueprint for your efforts.

2. **Mentorship and Coaching**:

- **Finding a Mentor**: Seek out mentors who have achieved the level of success you aspire to. Mentors can provide personalized guidance, advice, and support based on their experiences.

- **Coaching Programs**: Consider enrolling in coaching programs or hiring a business coach. Coaches can help you refine your strategies, set realistic goals, and stay accountable.

3. **Interviews and Podcasts**:

- **Expert Interviews**: Listen to interviews and podcasts featuring successful passive income earners. Platforms like YouTube, Spotify, and Apple Podcasts offer a wealth of content where experts share their knowledge and experiences.

- **Q&A Sessions**: Participate in live Q&A sessions or webinars where you can ask questions and get direct feedback from successful individuals.

Adapting Your Strategies as Needed

1. **Monitoring Performance**:

- **Regular Reviews**: Regularly review the performance of your passive income streams. Use analytics and performance metrics to assess what's working and what isn't.

- **Key Metrics**: Focus on key metrics such as ROI, conversion rates, and engagement levels. Tracking these metrics helps you understand the effectiveness of your strategies.

2. **Flexibility and Agility**:

- **Being Open to Change**: Be open to changing your strategies based on performance data and market conditions. Flexibility is crucial in adapting to new opportunities and overcoming challenges.

- **Experimentation**: Experiment with new approaches and strategies. Testing different methods can reveal more effective ways to achieve your goals.

3. **Feedback and Iteration**:

- **Gathering Feedback**: Collect feedback from your audience, customers, or peers. Their insights can highlight areas for improvement and new opportunities.

- **Iterative Improvements**: Implement changes incrementally and iteratively. Small, continuous improvements can lead to significant long-term gains.

Example Table: Continuous Learning and Adaptation Strategies

Strategy	Description	Benefits
Staying Informed	Follow industry news, read books, take online courses	Keeps you updated on new opportunities
Learning from Success Stories	Study case studies, seek mentorship, listen to podcasts	Provides practical insights and inspiration
Adapting Strategies	Regular performance reviews, be flexible, gather feedback	Ensures relevance and effectiveness

Case Study: Adapting to New Opportunities

Consider the case of John, an entrepreneur who initially focused on affiliate marketing for passive income. Over time, John noticed a decline in his affiliate revenue due to changes in search engine algorithms and increased competition. Instead of sticking rigidly to his original strategy, John decided to diversify his income streams.

He started by investing in real estate, which provided a stable and reliable income. John also explored creating online courses based on his expertise in digital marketing. By staying informed about market trends and learning from other successful earners in the industry, he adapted his strategies to include multiple income streams. This diversification not only compensated for the decline in affiliate marketing income but also significantly increased his overall passive income.

Continuous learning and adaptation are vital for sustaining and growing your passive income. By staying informed about new opportunities, learning from successful passive income earners, and adapting your strategies as needed, you can ensure your efforts remain effective and aligned with evolving market conditions. These practices will help you build a robust and diversified portfolio of passive income streams, leading to long-term financial stability and growth.

10.5 Creating a Balanced Life

Achieving financial independence through passive income is a significant milestone, but it's equally important to balance your income-generating activities with your personal life. This section explores strategies for balancing passive income activities with personal life, avoiding burnout, and enjoying the benefits of financial independence.

Balancing Passive Income Activities with Personal Life

1. **Time Management**:
   - **Prioritization**: Prioritize tasks based on their importance and urgency. Use tools like the Eisenhower Matrix to categorize tasks and focus on what matters most.
   - **Scheduling**: Create a balanced schedule that allocates time for work, personal activities, and rest. Tools like Google Calendar or Trello can help you organize and track your activities.

2. **Setting Boundaries**:
   - **Work Hours**: Establish clear work hours and stick to them. Avoid letting passive income activities spill over into personal time.

- **Physical Space**: Designate a specific area for work. Having a separate workspace helps create a mental boundary between work and personal life.

3. **Delegation and Automation**:

- **Outsourcing**: Delegate tasks that do not require your direct involvement. Hire virtual assistants or freelancers to handle routine tasks.
- **Automation Tools**: Use automation tools for repetitive tasks. For example, use social media scheduling tools like Hootsuite or Buffer to automate your content posting.

4. **Quality Time**:

- **Family and Friends**: Make time for family and friends. Building and maintaining strong relationships is essential for a balanced life.
- **Personal Hobbies**: Engage in hobbies and activities that you enjoy. Pursuing interests outside of work can provide a refreshing break and enhance overall well-being.

Avoiding Burnout

1. **Recognizing Signs of Burnout**:

- **Emotional Signs**: Look out for signs such as feeling overwhelmed, irritable, or constantly stressed. Emotional exhaustion is a key indicator of burnout.
- **Physical Signs**: Pay attention to physical symptoms like chronic fatigue, headaches, or sleep disturbances. These can be signs that your body needs a break.

2. **Preventative Measures**:

- **Regular Breaks**: Take regular breaks throughout the day to rest and recharge. The Pomodoro Technique, which involves working for 25 minutes followed by a 5-minute break, can be effective.

- **Healthy Lifestyle**: Maintain a healthy lifestyle with a balanced diet, regular exercise, and adequate sleep. Physical health directly impacts mental well-being.

3. **Stress Management Techniques**:

- **Mindfulness and Meditation**: Practice mindfulness and meditation to reduce stress and improve focus. Apps like Headspace and Calm can guide you through meditation exercises.
- **Deep Breathing**: Use deep breathing exercises to calm your mind and body. Techniques such as diaphragmatic breathing can help reduce stress levels.

Enjoying the Benefits of Financial Independence

1. **Freedom to Pursue Passions**:

- **Personal Projects**: Use your financial independence to pursue personal projects or passions that you may have previously set aside. This could include creative endeavors, travel, or learning new skills.
- **Volunteer Work**: Engage in volunteer work or philanthropic activities. Giving back to the community can provide a sense of fulfillment and purpose.

2. **Lifestyle Choices**:

- **Flexible Living**: Enjoy the flexibility that comes with financial independence. Whether it's working from different locations, taking extended vacations, or simply having more control over your daily schedule, flexibility can enhance your quality of life.
- **Experiences Over Possessions**: Focus on creating meaningful experiences rather than accumulating material possessions. Experiences such as traveling, attending events, or spending time with loved ones can bring lasting happiness.

3. **Continual Growth and Learning**:

- **Personal Development**: Invest time in personal development. This could include taking courses, reading books, or attending workshops. Continual growth ensures that you remain engaged and motivated.
- **Networking**: Build and maintain a network of like-minded individuals. Networking can lead to new opportunities, collaborations, and friendships.

Example Table: Balancing Work and Personal Life Strategies

Strategy	Description	Benefits
Time Management	Prioritize tasks, create a balanced schedule	Improved productivity, less stress
Setting Boundaries	Establish clear work hours, designate a workspace	Better work-life balance, increased focus
Delegation and Automation	Outsource tasks, use automation tools	More free time, reduced workload
Quality Time	Spend time with family and friends, engage in hobbies	Enhanced relationships, better mental health
Recognizing Burnout	Identify emotional and physical signs of burnout	Early intervention, reduced risk of burnout
Preventative Measures	Take regular breaks, maintain a healthy lifestyle	Increased energy, improved well-being

Strategy	Description	Benefits
Stress Management Techniques	Practice mindfulness, deep breathing exercises	Lower stress levels, improved focus
Freedom to Pursue Passions	Engage in personal projects, volunteer work	Greater fulfillment, sense of purpose
Lifestyle Choices	Enjoy flexible living, focus on experiences	Enhanced quality of life, lasting happiness
Continual Growth and Learning	Invest in personal development, build a network	Ongoing motivation, new opportunities

Case Study: Balancing Life and Passive Income

Consider the case of Sarah, a successful blogger who generates significant passive income from her website. Initially, Sarah struggled to balance her work with her personal life, leading to burnout. She decided to implement several strategies to regain balance.

Sarah started by setting clear work hours and creating a dedicated workspace in her home. She also hired a virtual assistant to handle routine tasks like email management and social media updates. By delegating these tasks, she freed up more time for herself.

Sarah incorporated regular breaks into her schedule and started practicing mindfulness meditation to manage stress. She also made a conscious effort to spend more time with her family and pursue hobbies like painting and hiking.

These changes not only improved Sarah's well-being but also enhanced her productivity. She was able to maintain a healthy balance between her passive income activities and personal life, ultimately enjoying the benefits of financial independence.

Creating a balanced life is essential for sustainable success in building passive income. By effectively managing your time, setting boundaries, avoiding burnout, and enjoying the benefits of financial independence, you can achieve a fulfilling and well-rounded life. These strategies will help you maintain motivation, productivity, and overall happiness as you pursue your passive income goals.

Appendix: Summary and Practical Guidelines for Building Passive Income

Building a successful and sustainable passive income stream is a multifaceted endeavor that requires careful planning, consistent effort, and the right mindset. This appendix provides a concise summary of the key points covered in this book and offers practical guidelines to help you navigate your passive income journey.

Summary of Key Points

1. **Understanding Passive Income**:

- **Definition and Importance**: Passive income is money earned with minimal ongoing effort. It is crucial for achieving financial independence and stability.

- **Types of Passive Income**: Includes investments, real estate, online ventures, and more. Each type has its pros and cons, and the best choice depends on individual circumstances and preferences.

2. **The Right Mindset**:

- **Growth Mindset**: Embrace a growth mindset that views challenges as opportunities for learning and growth.

- **Resilience**: Develop resilience to overcome setbacks and persist through difficulties.

- **Patience and Long-Term Vision**: Understand that building passive income takes time and requires a long-term perspective.

3. **Practical Steps to Building Passive Income**:

- **Setting Clear Goals**: Define specific, measurable, achievable, relevant, and time-bound (SMART) goals.

- **Education and Skill Development**: Continuously educate yourself and develop the necessary skills for your chosen passive income streams.

- **Strategic Planning and Execution**: Create a detailed action plan and execute it diligently. Monitor progress and adapt strategies as needed.

4. **Maintaining Balance and Avoiding Burnout**:

- **Time Management**: Prioritize tasks, set clear work hours, and use tools to manage your time effectively.

- **Work-Life Balance**: Ensure that your passive income activities do not overshadow your personal life. Make time for family, friends, and hobbies.

- **Health and Well-being**: Maintain a healthy lifestyle with regular exercise, a balanced diet, and adequate sleep. Practice stress management techniques like mindfulness and meditation.

5. **Continuous Learning and Adaptation**:

- **Stay Informed**: Keep up with market trends, new opportunities, and industry developments.

- **Learn from Others**: Study the success stories of other passive income earners and seek mentorship or coaching.

- **Adapt Strategies**: Regularly review and adapt your strategies based on performance data and feedback.

Practical Guidelines for Building Passive Income

1. **Start Small and Scale Gradually**:

- Begin with manageable projects that require minimal investment. As you gain experience and confidence, gradually scale up your efforts.

2. **Diversify Your Income Streams**:
   - Don't rely on a single source of passive income. Diversify your portfolio to mitigate risks and increase overall stability.

3. **Leverage Technology and Automation**:
   - Use technology and automation tools to streamline processes and reduce manual effort. This can include using scheduling tools for social media, automated email marketing, and property management software.

4. **Invest in Quality**:
   - Whether it's creating content, investing in real estate, or developing digital products, always prioritize quality. High-quality offerings attract more customers and yield better long-term returns.

5. **Monitor and Optimize**:
   - Regularly track the performance of your passive income streams using analytics and key performance indicators (KPIs). Identify areas for improvement and optimize your strategies accordingly.

6. **Build a Support Network**:
   - Connect with like-minded individuals, join professional associations, and participate in forums. A strong support network can provide valuable advice, resources, and motivation.

7. **Stay Patient and Persistent**:
   - Recognize that building passive income is a marathon, not a sprint. Stay patient, remain persistent, and keep your long-term vision in mind.

Final Thoughts

Embarking on the journey to build passive income requires a blend of strategic planning, continuous learning, and a resilient mindset. By following the principles outlined in this book and consistently applying the practical guidelines provided, you can create sustainable passive income streams that lead to financial independence and a balanced, fulfilling life.

Remember, the path to passive income is not without its challenges, but with dedication, adaptability, and a positive mindset, you can achieve your financial goals and enjoy the freedom and security that come with passive income. Stay motivated, keep learning, and persist in your efforts, and the rewards will follow.

Thank you for taking the time to read this book and embark on your journey to building passive income. Your dedication to achieving financial independence is truly inspiring. If you found this guide helpful, we would greatly appreciate it if you could leave a review on Amazon. Your feedback not only helps us improve but also assists other readers in finding valuable resources. Thank you for your support, and here's to your future success!

www.ingramcontent.com/pod-product-compliance
Lightning Source LLC
Chambersburg PA
CBHW050202230526
45470CB00001B/197